The Rising Workbook
How to Create Your Own Rising

Jeff Selver

Copyright © 2024 by Jeff Selver

All rights reserved.

No part of this publication may be reproduced, distributed, or transmitted in any form or by any means, including photocopying, recording, or other electronic or mechanical methods, without the prior written permission of the publisher, except in the case of brief quotations embodied in critical reviews and certain other non-commercial uses permitted by copyright law. For permission requests, write to the publisher, addressed "Attention: Permissions Coordinator," at the website below.

Printed and bound in the United States of America

ISBN: 9798878928960

www.jeffselver.com

To my Blessed Guru
The Great Masters
The Elder, my "Dolphin Twin"
The great Guru of the Galaxy, the Leader
And my beloved Kalika.

All words of the Guru are reprinted with permission and kindness because truth is free for all.

Table of Contents

How to Use This Workbook 1

Do We Really Know Who We Are? 5

    We Are Not the Body 9

    Our Inner Architecture: The Relationship Between Body, Mind, and Consciousness 13

    Is There Evidence for God? 15

    The Source of Our Consciousness 20

The Power of a Meditation Practice 25

    A Guide to Meditation 26

    Our Inner Architecture: Discerning the Voice of the Mind and the Voice of the Heart 34

    Being State 42

The Ocean of the Mind 45

    The Symbolic Self 45

    The Power of the Present 53

    Observing our Thoughts 56

Intuition & The Dimensionality of Consciousness 84

    How Consciousness Is Interpreted by the Brain 86

    The Energy of Our Body 89

    Sensing and Feeling With Our Being 92

    Opening Ourselves to Dimensionality 97

Detachment 112

The Rising 124

    The Five Keys to Enlightenment 126

    The Dimensions of the Universe Exist in the Incomprehensible Unity of Love 140

    Communicating with Source 147

We Are Creator Beings With the Power to Create Reality Through Visioning 152

    How to Vision 152

    Visioning the Life You Desire: Part 1 - We Are Creator Beings 160

    Visioning the Life You Desire: Part 2 - Finding Your Purpose 167

    Visioning the Life You Desire: Part 3 - Building and Manifesting the Vision 177

   The Completed State 194
There Is No Rising 195
Living in the World but Not of It 219
References 221

How to Use This Workbook

We truly are on the cusp of a new reality, and it is Beings from another dimension that will bring it upon us. The impetus for this workbook is to help us be ready.

In my 24th contact event, I witnessed through a hologram of the Earth that an electromagnetic field change would overcome the planet, a new frequency if you will, which would then affect human Consciousness, requiring us to understand our Source, our spiritual nature. And in my 25th contact event, the Elder urged me, upon releasing my memories, to "teach" what I experienced with them. These were the subconscious impetuses that ushered me to formulate this workbook.

Yet, since those memories have been brought to light I have come to the conclusion that for the human to live in this new world and operate the Grey alien technology, they need to understand the basic fundamentals of spirituality; ideas like Unity, learning to control the emotional mind, and being able to go beyond it, and an awareness of our dimensional capabilities. As the line that graces the back of *The Rising: And the Alien Plan to Build an Enlightened City on Earth;*

"It's not to dominate you. It's to change to societal structures that benefit you, and to change to societal structures that benefit nature. There are ways that are very advanced for a society to coexist, but they are reorientations of your sense of Self because they involve consciousness technology."

This workbook will create that reorientation of your sense of Self to operate their consciousness technology.

This workbook is designed to be an encyclopaedia of meditations, exercises, spiritual writings, and quotes from famous authors, Gurus, Masters, and spiritual scriptures, for readers with all levels of experience. You could read it front-to-back, skimming through the exercises and letting them percolate within you, or you could spend the time doing the exercises in order and experience the linear development, or you could pick and choose what exercises you desire.

This workbook is meant to accompany you in life, just as these trusted meditations and exercises have done for myself. True spiritual growth is like peeling an onion, with deeper layers being exposed over time, not only through practice, but also through life circumstances. You may read this book fully and apply ideas, and then come back to it months or even years later and get more out of it.

What lies before you is modelled after how the Beings created the Rising. Below are the chapter titles of this book with their connection to my story as it's laid out in *The Rising: The Alien Plan to Build an Enlightened City on Earth.*

Do We Really Know Who We Are? -

Theory and practice are two aspects of every branch of knowledge. Of these two, the former pertains to the intellectual grasp and clarification while the latter to the translation of it into action. One is pure science and the other, applied science.
  -Swami Chidbavanunda, commentary on the Bhagavad Gita

Spirituality starts with theory, with learning intellectually what you are, which creates the direction for the practice.

It was just after the publication of my first edition of *The Rising* did I reflect that the Beings followed this exact same tenant. With my exposure to the white room, I was shown who and what I am, which created the direction for the Rising.

Obviously, I can not provide you a white room experience, but I can show your intellect the science that demonstrates what you really are - a long living spiritual energy form connected to a unified field force. A firm grasp in what you are and what is possible opens the door to spirituality. That is what the chapter *Do We Really Know Who We Are?* will do.

The Power of a Meditation Practice - An additional detail of my story that never made it into *The Rising* was for several weeks leading up to, and also directly after, the 8th contact event on Hornby Island, I had several synchronicities, messages from the Universe if you will, to begin a meditation practice. People placed at the right moment, in several different occasions, were teaching me to meditate. Unfortunately, I made an excuse that I wasn't comfortable meditating in my car, and it was too cold outside to find a proper spot. It was only after I met my Guru, when I committed to a regular meditation practice, did my eyes open to just how beneficial it can be in someone's life. All these years later, I look back at travelling with a small tinge of regret that I didn't try harder to begin a meditation practice, as it would have surely helped me.

Now that I rely on a daily meditation practice, I recommend it from the beginning of this workbook. And I can say without a doubt that it's required to experience the higher echelons of Consciousness.

The Ocean of the Mind - In the fourth contact event, the Elder used a device to show me how my thoughts, those of my teenage need to conform, obstructed my spirit. Presently, this demonstrates to me that the mind needs to resolve its issues before attempting to achieve higher states of awareness, which is what this chapter addresses. Doing so prepares us for our dimensional awareness.

Intuition & the Dimensionality of Consciousness - After the fifth contact event, I began having "psychic" events, premonitions, energy experiences, and past life awareness, the topics of which are covered in this chapter.

Detachment - The main premise of the book that initiated the Rising was detachment, which gets explored in this chapter.

The Rising - I then provide you an experience of your own Source - God. This is the God realisation chapter

We Are Creator Beings With the Power to Create Reality Through Visioning - When I left to begin a life of travelling I began to put into practice my own ability to Vision, manifesting in the physical world exactly what I needed. This chapter brings all the practices together in the book, to provide you with your own experience of Visioning and manifesting it into reality.

We Are Creator Beings

The grand spiritual message from my experience with the aliens is that we are Creator Beings. That life, at its core, is a game of creation, and therefore all of our struggles arise from not knowing this.

The Twin mentioned to me that our freedom is in believing…

…in the unlimited potential of the higher power and the unlimited freedom of the soul…

Since we are Creators, it is therefore also a book about personal responsibility, connecting to our power, learning about love, and creating exactly what you want in life. When you create what you want in life, you then understand your Source.

True enlightenment is not something you stumble upon, but something grown, born of perspective and experience. It is a process. We are working to embody our spirits in physical form, that is the purpose of life, and that takes time, as the brain and body become accustomed. You can't know your Source until you experience yourself as Source, and this workbook contains all the principles to help you do that in our challenging times.

The Vedic System

Many years ago I had a dream I was reading the ancient Vedic text the Bhagavad Gita, which is written in the ancient language of Sanskrit. In this dream the Sanskrit words contained bright white light that penetrated my eyes, going directly into my heart. Since, I have had great reverence for the words of the Bhagavad Gita, and Vedic philosophy.

Spiritual truths exist beyond human comprehension; above systems of beliefs, and religions. Yet some spiritual systems and modes help us by explaining this greater reality in ways which give us an understanding of the forces beyond. For this reason I have fallen prey to Vedic philosophy.

Vedic philosophy is the origins of the Hindu and Bhuddistic way of life, and roots itself in a scientific and psychological system to awaken Source within. I have connected with it as the most effective human modality for describing spirituality. So Vedic philosophy will be throughout my writings.

I also have a Master, a SadGuru, meaning a True Guru. The voice of Universal love can be hard to hear when our minds only know parental and romantic love, yet a true Master demonstrates true Universal love. He has shown me in confused times, and in weakness, what the voice of the Universe really says. I will refer to my Guru throughout this book, as I would be nowhere without him.

So as you embark on your own journey, as the Elder said to me in my first contact event;

Keep your heart and mind open to learn new things.

Raising your level of belief will open the door to a world which was once thought to be fanciful magic, but can now be turned into an experience, which becomes a truth of the Self.

May you experience your unlimited potential with the higher power and the unlimited freedom of your soul.

Satyanaam
Jeff Selver, MBA

So that leads us to our first point;

1) Reality is an undivided whole

This phrase can sound like a hippie-dippy term, but in truth, it is from the Copenhagen Interpretation, home of the physics standard created around the principles of quantum reality. What this means is that the Source is underneath everything, and everything is interconnected in wholeness, i.e. Unity.

Now, to refer back to our computer simulation, the image itself appears three-dimensional, as if the car is going to drive towards a city, but we know that the image isn't three-dimensional, it's a two-dimensional flat screen generating the illusion that there is three-dimensional depth.

Time doesn't exist in the simulation either because even though you travel and there is perceived time, you will turn off the video game, it will reboot, and start from the beginning. So, time and space are actually illusions in this video game and only exist relative to the observer. Quantum reality says the same thing, that time and space are the illusions of the world around us. The experiments show that all timeframes and all points of space are available at once. This is hard to swallow but is the true nature of the Universe.

This leads us to our second point;

2) The Universe, at its source, contains all space and all time.

The constant state of our existence that sees movement through space and time is the illusion. Space and time are not constants in the Universe, awareness is. This is a very powerful point that we'll connect with later.

Lastly, in the video game, we can see off to both the left and right, giving the impression of wide landscapes, but we know this is only a computer-generated image and that past the screen they do not exist. The computer only generates the image of the city, road, or landscape once the frame of reference points in that direction, otherwise, if it does not, then objects in the periphery do not get created.

Again, in quantum physics this is how they are saying the Universe is created, by observation.

3) We create what we observe, and the Universe is observer created.

It is called *the observer effect* - the choice of the experiment determines the prior state of the electron, as if it is aware that it will be observed in the future, therefore predetermining its state. It is recognized in quantum physics that before observation matter does not exist, and lives in an interaction with consciousness, therefore defining the Universe as subjective.

If this blows your mind, it should.

travel instantaneously across it, read that, faster than the speed of light. Or in other words, two pieces of matter can influence each other and don't have to be in their locale. This is now defined as a true property of the nature of the Universe.

Yet, instant correspondence between two particles separated by unlimited distance in space only makes sense if all points in our Universe are equal distance to its source, the thing that's generating the Universe. Every molecule, proton, photon, everything, is in immediate touch with the thing that is creating it, and this is the same for the computer game. Each pixel generating the image is up against the processor. Each and every pixel is equal distance to its source, just like the world around you right now.

Take a moment to look at the world around you, the tables and chairs, or whatever you're looking at, and understand that every single point, every atom, and every little piece of everything, is instantly connected to the thing that's generating it, that's creating it. The Source is there right now, around you.

It therefore shouldn't be surprising that some of the more mysterious properties of quantum reality were first discovered by Albert Einstein. In his first research paper ever published, *On a Heuristic Viewpoint Concerning the Production and Transformation of Light* (1905), his theory of the "photoelectric effect" pointed to a new discovery of a property of the Universe; that every particle may be described as either a particle or a wave, called wave-particle duality.

It was Niels Bohr, Max Plank, Werner Heisenberg, and Erwin Schrodinger who would create a larger hypothesis, based on the math of the "photoelectric effect," that the Universe was in fact an illusion, at least on the smallest level, the quanta, and was influenced by the observing consciousness - that the nature of the Universe was in fact subjective, not objective. Science is founded in the reality that the Universe is objective, that its physics operates regardless of the observer, so it was seen as preposterous that we are impacting, in some inconceivable way, the world around us through observation.

Einstein himself spent 28 years trying to find an overarching unified theory which would demonstrate the Universe, outside quantum reality, was objective by nature, but he couldn't do it. One of the greatest minds of our time, with all his intelligence and scientific contributions to humanity, couldn't beat quantum reality.

After decades of mathematical conjecture, in 1982, Alan Aspec, after designing and building the complex hardware required, finally proved quantum reality real, and that the Universe had mysterious properties to it, such as non-locality - the instant correspondence between two particles separated by unlimited distance in space.

Ever since, scientists have been eager to disprove this seeming new truth that quantum reality is valid and therefore the Universe is subjective by nature. But when all the individual quantum mathematical realities, that are repeatedly proven in laboratory experiments, combine together, they show that the world around you is actually an illusion, a simulation. It might seem like a fanciful dream, but physics alone is arguing that the world we live in is subjective by nature, created by the one observing it. If this is true, where is the Universe coming from? Physicists don't know what creates the Universe and its apparent subjective nature. Science has its foundation in objective reality, so with this new direction it is in a crisis.

There are three points that quantum reality shows us about the nature of the Universe, which demonstrates we live in a simulation, that will be important to understand and internalize, to move forward.

To understand we live in a simulation we are going to use an actual simulation to demonstrate the similarities. Below is an image from a computer game. Imagine yourself in the image driving the car along the road lined with trees, in front are some buildings, implying a city, and a landscape panning out both to the left and right, as far as the screen will display.

Every point in the video game is being generated by a pixel from a computer screen, and those pixels are generated by a processor. Quantum reality is saying that the world we live in is similar, and it is explained in the concept of non-locality; that matter from one part of the Universe is connected to the matter in another part of the Universe without distance being an issue. Something unknown to our senses connects all matter in the Universe and information can

Do We Really Know Who We Are?

Do you know you are surrounded by mystery? I'm not just talking about looking up at the stars and marveling at the wondrous expanse of the Universe, but to consider the mystery that surrounds you in the apparent mundane events of your everyday world; washing the dishes, buying groceries, picking up the kids from school - you are surrounded by mystery.

Humans have been living in mystery since we have existed on Earth, and yet at the same time, throughout history, many have assumed all things to be discovered have been discovered, with the next steps of evolution being impossible to imagine.

Such as when a teacher named Philipp von Jolly told the young Max Planck, in 1874, that there was nothing more to discover in theoretical physics, and to not bother pursuing it as a career. Thankfully, he did not listen, as Planck would go on to be the originator of quantum theory.

Yet, there is a power in embracing the mystery of life and what we don't know, for it can humble us and drive our sense of wonder and curiosity. As Socrates wrote, *"The only true wisdom is in knowing you know nothing."*

Right now, those that humanity might deem the smartest minds amongst us are saying the world around you is an illusion, a hologram, and is not real; with titles of internet articles such as *Niel deGrasse Tyson thinks there's a 'very high' chance the universe is just a simulation*, or *Elon Musk says we may live in a simulation*.

This is the new frontier of quantum physics, and what is being discovered will leave you questioning reality. In short, we are being told that the matter that makes up our everyday lives is not real.

Maybe you've heard this before, or maybe it has caught your attention in the news. Yet, some people have not heard this before and rightfully question if this is so important then why haven't they heard more about it. In Nick Herbert's book, *Quantum Reality: Beyond the New Physics (1987)*, the author outlines the dilemma that scientists have in presenting this information to the public; they live in a world of mathematics, and it doesn't translate well to helping the average individual understand and internalize what quantum reality means to them personally.

It's important to understand why these clever scientists think that the Universe we live in is a simulation, and why they believe it is emerging from something nonphysical and beyond our senses. To do so can lead us to grasping the more mysterious and subtle properties of the Universe and unlock them for our own personal experience.

To understand the simulation theory, we need to know its origins and for that we look to Albert Einstein. Einstein, in our culture, is considered one of the greatest scientists of our time, having countless contributions to science, among them the theory of relativity, $E = MC2$, but also some that are seemingly mundane in comparison, which we take for granted, like why the sky is blue, the fusion process of the sun, and proving the existence of atoms.

Let us summarize;

1. Reality is an undivided whole.
2. The Universe, at its source, contains all space and all time (time and space are illusions).
3. We create what we observe, and the Universe is observer created.

We appear to be in a simulation, think the physicists, placed on a 3D screen, with its processor equal distances from every point in the Universe, and playing an active role in its manifestation with the world of objects brought forth by awareness, and space/time not being properties of nature, but perceptions. The Universe indeed obeys a nonhuman kind of logic.

We live in a non-reality and our sense of what is real is coming apart. I am reminded of Ernest Rutherford, the father of atomic physics in the early 1900's, when he discovered that atoms were made of 99% air, and suddenly saw the Universe around him not as he perceived it to be. He was so concerned with his new interpretation of the world that he was nervous his body was going to mistakenly float through the floor. His sense of what was real had literally been turned upside down. That is how we should be with this new reality.

Yet, what should we do with this information? If the world around us is not real, then what is?

We Are Not the Body

Presently, science cannot explain the origins of consciousness. The mechanical functions of the brain are well mapped out, yet its motivation remains a mystery. For neuroscientists it is called the *hard problem of consciousness*, because technically you should be an automaton; eating, protecting your children, and securing yourself in the world, but instead you might take up painting, go watch the sunset, or laugh with friends.

Even the origin of thoughts are not understood. When a brain is connected to a positron emission tomography (PET) scanner, the neurons generating the thought can be watched but we're not at the place where an Artificial Intelligence can map out those same neurons and then regenerate the thought in a computer.

Some, such as Stuart Hameroff, Roger Penrose, and Stuart Kauffman, are theorizing a possible quantum link to consciousness, as nano signatures have been found within organisms that contain similar structures to the neurons of the human brain, suggesting human awareness may be originating from something non-physical.

But it is the doctors who tell of patients that have near death experiences, that point to the true origins of consciousness.

People have been reporting near death experiences for thousands of years, yet, with the beginning of resuscitation medicine, in the 1960s and 70s, doctors witnessed more and more patients coming back from near death who reported leaving their body and going to another realm.

Psychiatrist Raymond Moody, coined the term Near-Death Experience (NDE) in his book *Life After Life* (1975), in which he detailed more than 100 people who survived "clinical" death but were subsequently revived.

Usually, they relate perceiving themselves from a perspective above or to the side of their physical body and describe accurately the conversations of the medical staff present in the room as well as the medical interventions that were performed on them. Given that they were clinically dead, how is this possible? Skeptics have raised objections to the credibility of these accounts by pointing out that they may be due to religious indoctrination. However, the phenomenon is remarkably consistent across cultures and religions and has been reported even by children and toddlers who were not exposed to religious doctrine.
-Dr. Thomas Verny; The Embodied Mind

The Division of Perceptual Studies at the University of Virginia has been applying the scientific method to the research of mediums, deathbed visions, reincarnation, and near-death experiences for over fifty years. Dr. Bruce Greyson, their former director (2002-2014) is quoted as saying;

When the heart stops, within twenty seconds or so, you get flatlining which means no brain activity. And yet people have near death experiences when they've been flatlined longer than that...Between 10-20% of people whose hearts actually stop will report these dramatic near-death experiences...Some have said it's the drugs, but the fewer drugs the more likely they are to have a NDE. Lack of oxygen in the brain - yet however from decades of research when the brain has lack of oxygen in fact people become belligerent and terrified of what's happening...There have been a number of medical explanations that have been proposed to explain what causes near-death experiences. I'm all in favour of that, being a doctor. I want to understand what's causing these things. Unfortunately, I don't think the explanations we have come up with so far help us understand things.
-Dr. Bruce Greyson on the Netflix Docuseries Surviving Death

The Neuropsychiatrist from University of Cambridge, Peter Fenwick has been studying near death experiences for over twenty years;

I'm frequently challenged by people who say, 'Ok, he's had a cardiac arrest. There's a little bit of brain working which you guys have all missed.' But this says that they don't really understand what consciousness is. You cannot maintain consciousness unless you have a highly organized brain. Believe you me, when the brain loses its oxygen, it doesn't organize itself...How can people be conscious when they are unconscious? It's an oxymoron, it's ridiculous, but that is

what the data is proving more and more. That of course is going to have some significance about our ideas of death. I mean, is it possible there is an expansion of consciousness when we die?
   -Dr. Peter Fenwick on the Netflix Docuseries Surviving Death

    The public, to a great extent, is unaware that the largest research on brain activity during cardiac arrest has found evidence that awareness does continue outside the body after flatlining. This research was conducted by Sam Parnia, a British associate professor of Medicine at the NYU Langone Medical Center where he is also director of research into cardiopulmonary resuscitation. Launched in 2008, and concluded in 2012, with 33 investigators, across 15 medical centers in the UK, Austria, and the United States, they tested consciousness, memories, and awareness during cardiac arrest, using special rooms designed with control methods. They determined if patients could accurately relate visual and auditory information that would have been impossible to gain had they not been outside their body. The results were 9% could be classified as having a near death experience, while 1% provided undeniable evidence by relaying information in the room that could only have been acquired had they not been in their body.
    Lastly, Dr. Jim Tucker, the current director of the Division of Perceptual Studies at UoV, has found evidence for reincarnation by applying the scientific method to his research.

The Hard Science of Reincarnation: All over the world, scholars studying reincarnation are making findings even skeptics have difficulty explaining.
   -Title of Vice article published March 31st, 2021.

    Tucker focuses on children who claim detailed memories of a past life, as they are less likely to have been exposed to their information in other ways. Using pictures personally associated with the claimed past life and not available on the internet, he provides where they lived, inside their place of residence, and of relatives, side by side a false image, i.e. a control method.

When we do these tests then we can look at statistically how likely it is for a child to choose five correct pictures by chance and of course that's pretty unlikely...I start from a point of skepticism, and I can doubt things at times like everyone else. I look for anything that is questionable or deceptive. But the longer I've been in this field, the more I've become convinced that there is more than just the physical world. That there is a larger reality.
   -Jim Tucker, M.D. on the Netflix Docuseries Surviving Death

    Many have experienced their consciousness beyond their body, whether it be from a near death experience, out of body experience, or past life awareness. I also experienced I was not the body in the white room, when it dissolved, and my awareness remained intact. Maybe you can identify with one of these types of experiences also.
    These glimpses of another reality show us that our awareness does not exist solely within the physical body, but only temporarily inhabits it.

You think you are your body, but you are not.
  -*The Mystic Book*

For humans this is a very high spiritual concept, as we are attached to the body, and identify with it fully.
So, where does that leave us if we are not the body?

> *Lead me from the unreal to the real,*
> *from darkness to light,*
> *from death to immortality.*
> -*Brihadaranyaka Upanishad 1.3.28*

If We Are Not the Body Then What Are We?

Being told we are not the body is the shock of truth we need, but it's more helpful to be told what we are, than to focus on what we are not. If we are not the body, then what are we?

What you are is a perfect awareness housed within and throughout physical tissue body.
  -*The Mystic Book*

In the white room, I was perfect awareness - unbridled, unconditioned, and pure. When my body reformed, I understood fully and completely that the perfect awareness that I am is all throughout my body, including through my hands and feet. I could even feel my awareness outside and around my body.
Your awareness is larger than you see with your eyes. This pure awareness is what governs the movements of your body.

Yet who you really are is a Quantum Dimensional Consciousness experienced as pure Being and pure feeling.
  -*The Mystic Book*

What is meant by Quantum Dimensional Consciousness?

Quantum: Quantum physics demonstrates the basic properties of the Universe are in no space and no time, or could be considered, all space and all time, as discussed previously. Within, you have access to this no/all space, no/all time, as it is a part of your own Consciousness.

Dimensional: When we look at the meaning of the word dimension, it is *a measurable extent of some kind, such as length, breadth, depth, or height,* as defined by The Oxford Dictionary (2023). Therefore, Consciousness can change its focus by levels and degrees within the properties of space and/or time, and also can be divided, without taking away from the whole. For example, you can remote view, as in peer to witness another space or location of the Universe simply with your Consciousness, but you can also create greater focus and send your entire ethereal body there and interact with others, thus you're increasing your awareness by focus, thus changing degrees, and therefore increasing your dimension of awareness. We can experience the same with time, which we will get into.

Consciousness: When we refer to Consciousness, we refer to the awareness you experience in its purest unconditional form. Soul isn't some far off energy, it is the awareness you use to perceive your world around you now.

Thus, **Quantum Dimensional Consciousness**.

The trick…was for Jonathan to stop seeing himself trapped inside a limited body…The trick was to know his true nature lives…everywhere at once across space and time.
  -Jonathan Livingston Seagull

  Like I was shown my Higher Self in the white room, you also have a Higher Self that is the designer of all your lives in the physical realm, understanding the specific purposes of each manifestation, and intelligently planning your evolution. Using the metaphor of a tree, you are the leaf, and the Higher Self is the branch, which is an offshoot in Unity with an even grander awareness, which is the Source of our Consciousness. When the human mind cannot hold nor conceive of the multidimensional Higher Self, then we project it as an outside force. When we find God in our hearts, we come to the Higher Self. I know for certain this Higher Self wants me to be it as much as possible; to embody it, to think like it, and act like it – this is what it means to embody God.

The Self, Shiva, is supremely pure and independent, and you can experience it constantly sparkling within your mind. It cannot be perceived by the senses, because it makes the senses function. It cannot be perceived by the mind, because it makes the mind think. Still, the Self can be known, and to know it we do not need the help of the mind or the senses.
  -Swami Muktananda; I am That

Our Inner Architecture: The Relationship Between Body, Mind, and Consciousness

  The Upanishads are a set of ancient Vedic scriptures, whose date of creation is largely contested, but most modern historians place them around 700-500 BC. They are typically thought of by the modern individual as a religious texts, yet, what is undisputed is that they are the first to understand and put into writing the fundamental truths of reality now being proven by quantum physicists; that reality is an undivided whole (Tat Tavum Asi - That thou Art), time and space are illusions (Kaivalya - the Absolute), and reality is observer created (Pragyanaam Brahma - Consciousness creates reality). No other culture, or religion, in the world made these statements first with such clarity as the Vedas.

What the ancient Upanishads actually are is a collection of wisdom handed down from those who spent hundreds if not thousands of years studying human enlightenment. They are very valuable in our present world, especially when one can rely on a Vedic Master to help interpret them.

The Vedic text the Katha Upanishad depicts a description of Self that helps us reframe our identity in this new quantum era, and from my entire experience with the aliens - the white room and the Rising - and overarching experience of Consciousness, this is the most accurate explanation of the Self I have found. It is described in the image below.

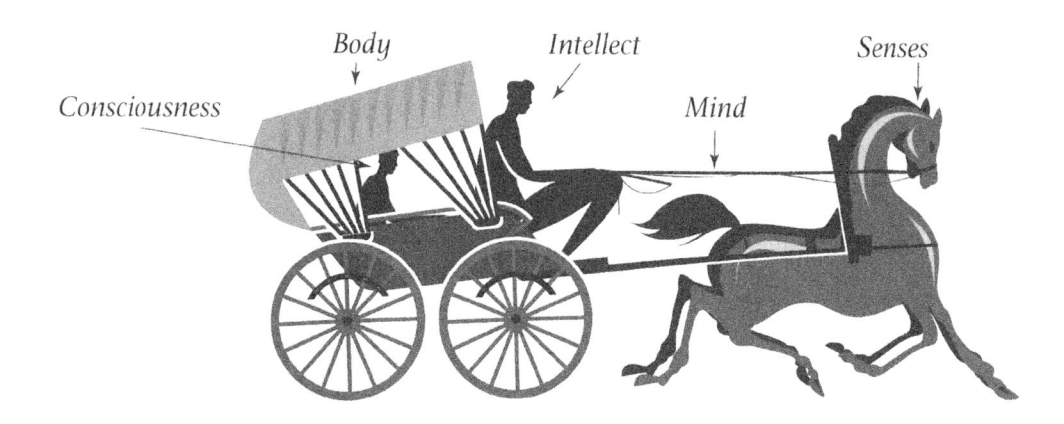

In this metaphor the chariot is the physical body, the rider is Consciousness, the driver is the intellect, the reins are the mind, and the horses are the five senses.

The first wisdom we gain from this metaphor is that our Consciousness is separate from our mind and is the source and power of the mind.

Yet who you really are is a Quantum Dimensional Consciousness experienced as pure Being and pure feeling.
   -*The Mystic Book*

Pure Being and pure feeling are of the heart. Our Consciousness is our heart, and the mind is a tool to be used by the heart. Throughout history we have identified ourselves with our mind, but instead, we are a heart that has a mind.

The second wisdom we gain is that the mind receives all of its information from the five senses, like a computer collecting data about the environment. It therefore acts like a repository of past information, while Consciousness is our true identity in the Absolute.

The intentions of our thoughts, words, and actions can be set from either of two places; the mind, from past information it has deduced, or from Consciousness in the present, or better put, from a greater understanding.

Consciousness is the rider, conforming to whatever the intellect chooses. Should you make a choice based on what has happened in the past or should you listen to your heart in the present?

Describing the mind as a repository of past information is not meant to indicate something less, as we need past information to drive our cars, conduct our professions, and live with our families. Yet when past information dictates our intentions and desire, or colours our experience of Consciousness, then we are choosing a Self that is less. A little later we will break all of this down to thoroughly understand it.

By identifying ourselves with Consciousness, with this metaphor of the chariot, we do not identify with our mind, or body, but with our heart.

Is There Evidence for God?

Is God real? Is there evidence for a unified field force that we are each connected to? Does the Universe respond to our expectations of it, therefore acting alive if we treat it as alive? Or is it all just a trick of the mind in which we create meaning out of random coincidences, and project onto a make-belief force the love and acceptance we wished we had received from our parents? What evidence could exist for God?

These are what I call the five evidences for God.

Evidence 1

Doctor Jessica Utts, professor of statistics at the University of California, Irvine, analyzed the statistical results of the controlled experiments of 10 laboratories conducting classified remote viewing research at the Stanford Research Institute. Remote viewing is the viewing of objects, vehicles, buildings, and even photographs, from a distance, with mental visualization.

There was enough validity with the program that the CIA used it for 20 years until the end of the Cold War, and Jimmy Carter spoke of its success in finding a downed soviet aircraft in Africa in 1978.

Essentially what Utts found was statistically the success rate was low - 1 in 3 - yet those who were successful, displayed a level of accuracy that was significant, beyond chance, and could not be explained as lucky guesses, proving remote viewing's validity. She concluded from her statistical analysis that there was a 1 in 10 billion chance participants could have successfully guessed the level of detail remotely viewed so consistently.

Other skeptics analyzing the data, such as Ray Hyman, agreed with her analysis, that there was overwhelming statistical evidence in favor of the human ability to remote view.

I think it implies that we need to get the physicists working on this. I think there really is something we don't understand about physics…I think we have great clues that we can do it over long distances and do it across time. Those are great clues that something is incomplete about our understanding of the Universe if we think of it as three dimensions plus time.
-Dr. Jessica Utts interview on Beach TV, March 26th, 2018

What the research discovered was that distance was irrelevant to the ability, that it is just as easy to remotely view something in Australia or China as it was to see something in your own backyard.

Also, sometimes, successful remote viewing is intertwined with precognition, where locations are seen with features not present until a couple days later. For example, a target is given and when successfully viewed it is a construction site. The viewer witnesses a crane that, at the time of the viewing, hasn't been installed yet, but then, a couple of days later, it is erected in the exact location it was seen.

Trying to understand what natural force allows humans to remote view, they placed participants in a submarine 500 miles out, and 500 feet down in the sea, to discern if it interfered with the ability, they also placed them in a Faraday cage to block electromagnetic fields, but whatever they did had no impact on the results.

A field that allows remote viewing through space and time, that has no distance or barriers, is the field of Universal Consciousness the ancients have talked about, and the quantum physicists are discovering, that you are connected to and can experience right now.

Evidence 2

As mentioned previously, evidence exists that humans live in a birth and death life cycle, and many people, including myself, have past life awareness. So, then the question can be asked; why would nature create a Consciousness with multiple recurring selves, each with their own pains, agonies, struggles, and hurts, unless there was a holistic psychological perspective that could encompass them all, a resolution that allowed us to not carry over every single issue that could arise in a given life, a grand view about pain, suffering, and the purpose of manifestation in physical reality.

This is the psychology of the Higher Self, of our own connection to God Consciousness, which takes a grander perspective of our emotional pains and issues. That there is a larger perspective in which our perceived pains are used for growth. A different way of seeing existence that heals us when we understand a larger reason for the pain's purpose. A perspective that resolves us so greatly that we make the choice ourselves to come back and do it all over again. These is the exact principles espoused of the Eastern tradition religions, such as Hinduism and Buddhism, which seeks to create a detachment from physical reality and the hardships we can endure, emphasizing an equilibrium of the mind through acceptance, forgiveness, and compassion.

Evidence 3

Neuroscientist Doctor Andrew Newberg and therapist Mark Waldman studied the brains of those who experience God, from all types of religions, and non-religions alike, including atheists, and wrote about their results in the book *How God Changes Your Brain* (2010). They found that the brain is uniquely designed to generate and perceive spiritual realities, that God is part of our Consciousness, and that the more you think about God, the more sensitive the brain becomes to subtle realms of experience. Intense contemplation of God permanently changes the structure of the parts of the brain that give rise to our sense of self, that builds our sensory perceptions of the world, and strengthens specific neurology that generates compassion, empathy, for others, social awareness, and peacefulness, all while subduing destructive emotions. This is of course as long as we are not believing in a God that is vindictive, punitive, or supports an "us vs them" mentality, all of which damages the brain.

Fascinatingly, Unity, one of the defining experiences of God, creates noticeable and remarkable differences in the brain. Those who meditated or who worshiped God have reduced activity in the parietal lobe, a part of the cortex involved with constructing our sense of self;

The parietal lobe, when active, gives us a sense of our self in relation to time, space, and other objects in the world...when activity in the parietal areas decreases, a sense of timelessness and spacelessness emerges. This allows the meditator to feel at one with the object of contemplation: with God, the universe, peacefulness, or any other object upon which he or she focuses.

We don't fully understand the reason for it, but it appears that a loss of self-consciousness enhances one's intention to reach specific goals. A loss of one's sense of self also appears to improve one's ability to perform a variety of tasks, with greater pleasure. In sports it's called being "in the zone," and in psychology, this state of optimal experience is called "flow."
    -*Newberg & Waldman; How God Changes Your Brain*

What Newberg and Waldman's research show is that Unity, spiritual states, and contemplation on God are not just beneficial for the brain, but natural as well.

Evidence 4

Would Visioning, which is the manifestation of our thoughts and feelings, not be our own greatest indicator of our own personal God power?

Many have experienced Visioning to be a real, but there is very little science to prove its existence. Yet, if we think of Visioning as the outward reflection of a thought or feeling with a convergence of a meaning making event in space and time, then the closest science would be that of coincidences.

Humans have always been baffled by coincidences, and many of us can think of a time in which a coincidence played a role in our life.

The biologist Paul Kammerer, who theorized the science of epigenetics long before his time, was also the first to study coincidences, organized their types, and believed there were only visible manifestations of a larger force, obeying a natural law. Writing a book on the subject in 1919, Albert Einstein has been quoted as saying his theories were "*by no means absurd.*"

Carl Jung, the Swiss psychoanalyst, working with Krammerer's research, took them seriously enough to document them with legitimate scientific enquiry as well, and coined the word "*synchronicity.*"

Some researchers subscribe to the fringe claim that invisible forces "*make things happen,*" such as psychiatrist Bernard Beitman, a psychiatry and neurobehavioral sciences professor at the University of Virginia, and a coincidence researcher, and the first since Carl Jung to systematize their study. He suspects an invisible network connects everyone and everything, and that humans transmit some unobserved energetic information, which other people then process or organize into emotion and behavior.

Just as sharks have ampullae in their skin that detect small electromagnetic changes to help them locate their prey ... it's plausible, maybe even probable, that humans have similar mechanisms that detect coincidences.
-Bernard Beitman

In terms of quantum reality, and if the Universe is a simulation, the concept of a subjective meaning making event, reflecting in space and time as a synchronicity, could make sense in terms of quantum entanglement; that two particles are connected regardless of distance.

Even though there may be no science to support Visioning, there is considerable evidence that when we build a Vision in which we believe to be real, the brain and body change as if it is already a reality. When you intensely imagine, the brain fully envelopes what it sees and begins to relate to your Vision as if it were an actual object in the world by increasing activity in the thalamus, part of the reality-making mechanism in the brain. The concept begins to feel more obtainable and real, and this is the first step in motivating other parts of the brain to take deliberate action.

Even if we don't think we're good at visualization, all thoughts including abstract concepts, such as peace, or God, are first processed in the visual centers in the cortex, telling us that the brain is built to envision every thought it has. **We create what we observe, and the Universe is observer created.** What you imagine is what you observe.

It therefore isn't hard to conceive of the next step; that a subjective, simulation-Universe responds to the projection of our Consciousness, beyond the brain.

Visioning is real, but our ability to affect our world is more subtle than we expect, all of which we will delve into later. When we understand Visioning is real, then the concept that we are God makes sense, as we are simply smaller versions of It. It is doing on a grand scale what we can do on a smaller scale - we are It, It is us.

Evidence 5

Can we find any evidence for an intelligent order to the Universe within the statistical probability that it would create life? There are still too many unknowns regarding how solar systems are created, and the circumstances needed for the chemical compounds of life to flourish on a planet, but if we're looking for an intelligent order in the statistical probability the Universe would create life, there are some interesting statistics to take note of.

The most abundant elements in the Universe are hydrogen, helium, and oxygen. Hydrogen and helium create stars, and we know, from the Kepler space telescope's observations, that for every star there will be at least one exoplanet. An intelligent order can then be glimpsed from a Universe that is designed to create stars, of which will create planets. One in five stars like Earth are going to have an Earth-size planet in the habitable zone; the zone within the solar system that is considered not too far or not too close to the sun which create the right conditions for life similar to our own. Based on Kepler's Data, there is a 95% chance that there is an Earth-like planet within 20-light years of our own solar system. That is a significantly high probability.

With the ingredients for water, hydrogen and oxygen, so abundant in the Universe, astrophysicists have found it is much more common in space than expected, including in our own solar system, with water found on the moon, and even Mercury.

Though space itself can be violent and chaotic, the stable conditions required for life can form naturally. As each planet is created, the heaviest elements move to the core, and if the planet is large enough, creating enough gravitational force towards the center, it will create a molten core, and if those elements are electrically conductible, such as iron, the sixth most common element in the Universe, then a magnetic field will be created.

A magnetic field, protecting the planet from solar radiation, will naturally create stability on the surface, allowing the lighter elements to rise, turning into gasses, and creating an atmosphere, which in turn will protect the surface against the bombardment of meteors and comets, creating more stability, making the conditions for life suitable.

It is interesting to note those in the field of chemistry, genetics, and astronomy, who believe, from all they know, that an intelligent order is involved in the creation of life on Earth.

Ilya Prigogine, chemist-physicist, and recipient of two Nobel Prizes in chemistry, in a Physics Today article titled *Thermodynamics of Evolution* (1972) wrote:

The statistical probability that organic structures and the most precisely harmonized reactions that typify living organisms would be generated by accident, is zero."

Professor Francis Crick, awarded the Nobel Prize for the discovery of DNA, in his book *Life Itself: Its Origin and Nature* (1982) wrote:

An honest man, armed with all the knowledge available to us now, could only state that in some sense, the origin of life appears at the moment, to be almost a miracle, so many are the conditions which would have had to have been satisfied to get it going.

The astronomer Fred Hoyle, in his book, *Evolution from Space: A Theory of Cosmic Creation* (1981) wrote:

The trouble is that there are about two thousand enzymes, and the chance of obtaining them all in a random trial is only one part in $(10^{20})^{2,000} = 10^{40,000}$, an outrageously small probability that could not be faced even if the whole universe consisted of organic soup.

The Universe, within a degree of variability, will create favorable conditions for life in the vastness of space. The Universe is meant to create life.

God is real and can be experienced, but it is subtle, beyond our comprehension, within and throughout.

I laugh when I hear the fish in the water is thirsty
-Kabir Sahib

The Source of Our Consciousness

You have no proper word in your world for the thing that you call God. Other labels associated with it are; the Great Mother, quantum field, Jesus, Mohammad, Yahweh, the Great Guru, Aware Universe, Source, etc. It is the Great Pulse. In this dialogue we will refer to That as Source, God, and Aware Universe as these, we feel, best describe it….Your human history has created concepts such as groveling and pleasing a person you deemed to be God. You still fight this historically created concept. Release your historical ego…
-The Mystic Book

Throughout history, the mind's inability to comprehend Source has led humans to create many different interpretations through religious institutions, based in different social, political, and historical contexts.

Humans, using our minds, have given human-like qualities to something vastly non-human, and outside the mind. It is Source because it is the source of our Consciousness, with which you are connected to through our awareness. Consciousness not only resides in Source, but it is also Source.

The idea that there is some sort of personality outside of us that is parent-like is not reality. Source and human are best analogized as a tree to a leaf, or ocean to the wave of the ocean, or flame to the spark of the flame. See Source as the tree, and you as the leaf playing out one individual experience amongst all of them. We are smaller versions of It; God-lets living out our existence within, with, and as Source. It is nature, an experience of energy, and does not hold concepts of judgment or morality.

When we know where we come from and who we are we move closer to our true potential and how we can use Source in our lives. Our loves, dreams, and desires are its reality and with it we can create them into manifested space and time, showing us that life can be a constant process of joy.

If it's not clear, we will not comprehend Source with our mind as its concepts don't make logical sense. Can a two-dimensional stickman contemplate the third dimension? Can us living in time and space understand how we can be connected to no time and no space? Yet, Source can be experienced by yourself without anyone else interpreting it for you. To do so, we must learn to let go of the mind.

What does eternity feel like? What does unlimited expanse feel like? What does freedom feel like? Take a second to contemplate the answers to these questions, as they will be in your heart, and not in your mind. This is Consciousness. Now deepen this awareness by thinking about when was the last time you felt in love with life? The Source is a loving experience of Unity, and sometimes it is accompanied by an experience of being larger than Self. Think about your own experience of Source. What does it feel like to you?

Source speaks to us all the time – daily. Perhaps you felt a voice within tell you a choice that was best to make. Maybe an image from your heart provided insight into a problem. Perhaps you felt a warmth that everything will be OK when you're having a bad day. If an event occurs that appears synchronistic and beneficial for you, try thinking of it as from your Higher Self, merged in the unified field of Source. Had an experience that seems like a message to you from a higher place? Try thinking of it as coming from Source.

Source is the power plant and you are the lightbulb.

You are Source

You find Source by trusting that the voice in your heart is its voice, that your feeling is its feeling. The voice of the heart is not emotion which is of the mind and is often in response to how we feel, all of which we will get into a little later. In essence, you are your Source when you are exactly who you are when coming from the heart, merged with your identity of you as One with Source. Its heart is my heart, my heart is Its heart; we share the One heart.

If we contemplate what it means to be in Unity with Source, then we come to a profound conclusion - Source experiences our lives with us - and this is the truth; the aware Universe is living your life through you, with joy. This is not something to fear, as morality or judgment do not exist in a place such as the Absolute - we are the judgers of our own lives. Life is the point.

The joy of creating and experiencing manifested space and time is the point. Awareness of the shared relationship with Source creates a powerful sense of security, as our pains are shared with it, therefore we can communicate to Source about our personal issues, and Source can respond, we just have to know how to listen, which we will get into a little later.

We are Multidimensional Beings

My teacher had been repeating the importance of imagination in understanding our spirit for years, but I didn't quite understand the teaching, until one day, I was listening to a CD of his in the shower when I finally understood how the past, present, and future are an illusion. This is what he said;

Close your eyes and think of the sofa in your living room. See the sofa in your living room, see its color. Now seat yourself in the center of the sofa, which is the most uncomfortable place. Feel the discomfort. Then go to the most comfortable part of the sofa, sit down, and feel the fabric. Get up from the sofa, stand up. Now open your eyes. Did you see it in the past? Did you see it in the future? Did you see it in the present? You didn't even see it in the present. In that moment there is no present. There is no present. By the time I say present, present is gone. And there is no past. So, when you vision, you don't vision in the past, you don't vision in the future, you don't vision in the present.
    -Maharaj

It finally hit me the brilliance of this teaching; the timelessness of imagination is the same place that I would build a Vision, in which I desire to manifest in the physical world, and it is also the same space I experienced awareness of past lives. That sense of timelessness is Consciousness, is the soul, is the Absolute, is the dimensional place beyond space and time. Thank you Guruji for this understanding!
    It might be helpful for yourself to spend a moment reflecting on the above exercise.

Your true identity, while simultaneously manifesting in space and time, also resides in a dimensional place beyond space and time.
    -The Mystic Book

That feeling of timelessness is the feeling of Consciousness. Time is an illusion, and only your Consciousness, which resides in timelessness, is real. This Consciousness, which the Vedas intuited thousands of years ago, is your quantum Self.

Consciousness does not live in the past, the present, or the future. It does not understand time and space. It is. It was never born, and it will never die. Consciousness is you and Consciousness is me. There was never a time that you were not and there will never be a time that you will cease to be. That is the feeling of Consciousness.
-Tulshi Sen; Ancient Secrets of Success for Today's World

The great realization in the white room was that I have been repeatedly living out lives in the birth and death life cycle, and I have since discovered that my history is massive. What does all this mean to me? That I am grander, and more magnificent, than I can comprehend.

You are not who you think you are, and your greatest joy is bringing who you really are into this world. We are a heart with a mind, not a mind with a heart. We are unlimited by nature, living in timelessness, and all those lives we have are being experienced right now, not in the past, and not later - Now.

You do not die; you continue to live and do so forever. Your current life is a blip in the cosmic timeline.

You are grander, and more magnificent, than you can comprehend. In truth, you are a multidimensional Being living out multiple lives, in multiple places, in multiple times all in the Now, all of which we will explore a little later.

The story of the cub that was raised by goats, as told by Tulshi Sen in his book *Ancient Secrets of Success for Today's World* (2007), explains this perspective well;

The Story of the Lion Cub Who Was Raised by Goats
How we deny our identity and stay ordinary.

One day a hunter killed a lioness and dragged it away. He did not know that she had a cub in the cave and left it there. The cub was helpless. There were some goats around who fell for the lion cub and brought up this cub as one of their own.

The lion cub grew up eating what the goats ate. It thought what the goats thought, it bleated as the goats bleated and it lived as a goat. It did not know anything better. It was happy and contented and scared of everything and survived on grass and leaves.

Then one glorious day a magnificent lion appeared on a hillock around where the goats were grazing and gave a loud roar. All the goats ran helter-skelter. The lion cub did not run. He felt a sense of kinship but did not know what it was. The cub looked up in amazement at this regal powerhouse and stood still. The Lion walked up to the cub and said, "Who are you? Where is your mother? And why do you eat grass and leaves?"

The slightly scared lion cub feeling a sense of frightened joy bleated, "I am a goat. These goats are my family. What else can I eat?"

The Lion roared with dismay and said, "You are a Lion, and you eat meat and not grass. Grass is for goats. And don't bleat, you roar." The Lion gave a roar again and the whole forest reverberated with the sound.

The lion cub bleated back and said, "No, I'm a goat. Can't you see?"

The Lion told the cub, "Come with me," and took him to a nearby pond. And then he told the cub, "Look at my face, and now look at the reflection of my face in the still pond."

The lion cub saw the majestic face of the Lion and then saw the reflection of that face in the pond. Then he saw his own reflection in the pond. He became still for a moment which felt like eternity, and then gave out a loud roar, "I am a Lion." The Universe resounded with a joyful cry. I am a Lion.

The Power of a Meditation Practice

The mind, which is a part of your body, takes on the characteristics of your physical environment, the planet your body is from, therefore the mind will only take you so far in understanding Universal truths.
-*The Mystic Book*

If the mind will only take us so far in understanding Universal truths, then how can we use it to get us to a place to be receptive to something greater than its comprehension? The answer is with meditation.

I have been practicing meditation for over twenty years, twice a day, once in the morning and once in the evening, at the recommendation of my teacher, and this is because the benefits of meditation have long been known.

First, we can access the deeper and subtle sensations of Consciousness with the power of focus and concentration.

Second, by giving the mind a concentrated focus in a meditative state it becomes removed from the present interpretation of our feeling, getting it "out of the way" so to speak, allowing a deeper experience of Self to occur. In essence, meditation neutralizes the mind so we can experience pure Consciousness.

Third, the type of meditation I will provide for you, which consists of breathing, focus, and mantra/word repetition, is documented, in the decades long study on meditation, as the most beneficial for your brain's neurology.

Focused breathing meditation, in numerous well-documented studies, reduces blood pressure, stress, regulates immunity, aging, cell decay, and replenishes the frontal lobe, which uses up a lot of energy in our everyday thinking.

The anterior cingulate becomes activated, which is a structure of the brain designed to regulate emotions, reducing anxiety and irritability, and countering the effects of depression, while enhancing social awareness, learning, and memory.

When meditation is combined with a mantra the effects in the brain only increase. Activity in the prefrontal cortex enhances an area of the brain involved in maintaining a clear, focused attention on a task. When the mantra is a concept or a goal, your brain begins to relate to it by increasing activity in the thalamus, part of the reality-making processor in the brain. Over time, the concept becomes fused with your identity.

We believe that meditation is particularly important for the brain because it counteracts our biological propensity to react to dangerous situations with animosity or fear. However, it also appears to make us more sensitive to the suffering of others, which may explain why those traditions that emphasize meditation are often involved in community charities and peacekeeping ventures.

Mantras...have been shown to have a distinct, powerful, and synchronous effect on the cardiovascular rhythms of practitioners...From a spiritual perspective, each mudra or mantra is associated with a theological or metaphysical idea, but from a scientific perspective, any form of repetitive movement or sound helps to keep the mind focused.
   -Newberg & Waldman; How God Changes Your Brain

Meditators, while not meditating, have higher levels of parietal activity in the brain, which are signs that meditation strengthens one's sense of self in the world, and the spiritual dimensions they experience. The increase of parietal activity is associated with alertness, empathy, the ability to resonate with other people's feelings and thoughts, and increased Consciousness.

I can say personally that I don't believe we can achieve the level of understanding about our connection to the Universe, one that allows us to live a complete and fulfilled life, without meditation. Its history starts with the Vedas, and its purpose was to self-realize that Source is inside you.

Therefore, what follows is a Vedic style of meditation, as guided by my teacher, broken down into a descriptive outline of five steps to help you conduct it properly.

The restraint of the modifications of the mind-stuff is Yoga. Then the Seer (Self) abides in Its own nature.
   -The Yoga Sutras of Patanjali 1.2

If you can control the rising of the mind into ripples, you will experience Yoga.
   -Swami Satchidananda; Commentaries to The Yoga Sutras of Patanjali

A Guide to Meditation

1) Posture (*Asana*)

Asana means seat or posture in Sanskrit. With meditation it refers to a posture that allows for concentration. We want to choose a posture that makes us comfortable enough that we don't focus on the body and can remain steady. From experience, I find the half lotus position the most comfortable for those who know it. To describe it, sit cross legged and place your right leg on top of the left so your right foot is on top of your left knee. This position shifts the pelvis, allowing it to easily straighten the back, making breath easy to focus on. We should see the body, neck and head erect, which makes the spinal cord vertical. It is in this posture that harmonized breathing takes place, good thoughts come naturally, and concentration on a point of focus becomes easy. It is important to feel comfortable and not strain yourself in any way. If there is strain, make an adjustment to feel comfortable.

If sitting cross legged is hard on your body, then sit in a chair with your back straight and feet flat on the floor.

Next, place your hands on your knees, palm down (not palm up which is commonly seen in pictures of people meditating on the internet) and touch your index finger and your thumb together. This is called a *mudra*, the details of which we will not go into here, but just know our body is sensitive to the flow of natural electrical energies, and this hand posture creates a current that is grounding.

2) Breath

It is said: adau bhagavan shabda rashib, "God originally manifested as sound." This primordial sound is called spanda, or vibration. It created the universe and still pervades everywhere, continually vibrating. Even modern physicists agree that there is a vibration reverberating ceaselessly at the center of the universe. This vibration is the source not only of the universe, but of our entire being, and it pulses within us.
-Swami Muktananda; I am That

Everything around us is in rhythm, is pulsating; the sound wave carried to your ear is oscillating up and down, the cells in the air around you have a life cycle. And this expands outwards to the cycle of the weather, the seasons of the planet, the rhythm of the solar system, and the spinning of the galaxy. Everything is moving, everything is in rhythm, everything is in a cycle, everything is pulsating. This is the pulse of God, and we can experience this grand pulse within us as our breath.

Meditation's foundation is breath; full and natural breaths. Breathe into the belly as if you're pushing out your belly button, and notice the pause, then release by bringing the belly in. In meditation workshops, when demonstrating how to breathe, I will often use the video of a slow-motion pendulum. When a pendulum is slowed down, as it hits the top of the swing, it pauses before it falls and starts the momentum in the other direction - our breath should emulate this.

Breathe in and out through the nose.

We don't want our breathing to be mechanical or forced, so knowing what to emulate, let go of thinking about your breath. It's important to make sure your breathing is natural and rhythmic but not forced.

When you begin to breathe this way, do you notice any differences inside yourself? Breath and mentation are highly connected. If you have ever noticed, when you are agitated the emotions create hindrances in your breathing. It is very easy to make one calm by focusing on breath, on the rhythm in breathing.

The supreme Shakti, whose nature is to create, constantly expresses Herself upward in the form of exhalation, and downward in the form of inhalation. By steadily fixing the mind on either of the two spaces between the breaths, one experiences the state of fullness of Bhairava (Param Brahma - God)
    -Vijnana Bhairava v24

Hamsa is the sound of your breath and translated from Sanskrit it is "That I am". Breathe in hearing *Ham* and breathe out hearing *Sa*. Experience this meditation by repeating *Ham* within, not out loud, as you breathe in, and *Sa* within, not out loud, as you breathe out.

Hamsa is the natural mantra. There are many mantras that you repeat with your tongue, many mantras that you repeat on the beads of a japa mala. But Hamsa is not like these. Hamsa mantra emanates spontaneously from within you, it repeats itself naturally along with your breathing. For this reason, it is called your own mantra or the mantra of the Self. The Vedas have given a high place to this mantra. The Tantra Shastras, too, have given it an important position. The great beings, the Siddhas, sing of it in their poetry.

When the breath comes in with the sound ham and merges inside, there is a fraction of a moment which is completely still and free of thought. This is madhyadasha, the space between the breaths. This is where you have to focus in meditation. To focus on that space is the highest meditation and the highest knowledge. That still space between the breaths, that space where no thoughts exist, is the true goal of the mantra.

It is a miraculous space. It is aham vimarsha, the inner pulsation of Consciousness. It is from this space that all words arise and subside. It is this space without form which pulls the apana inside and which pushes the prana out. This space where ham merges inside, before sa has arisen, is the space of God, of supreme Consciousness, of the Self. The place where sa merges outside is equally the place of God. So, realize that moment of the merging of the two syllables. If you come to know that moment, if you become established in it, you experience the truth.

...In that space there are no thoughts, no imaginings, no feelings. It is completely free of forms and attributes. In that state there is no pain, no pleasure, no dullness, no ignorance. That is the state of the supreme Truth. It is turiya, the transcendental state.
    -Swami Muktananda; I am That

The name of God in the Bible, as given to Moses, is *I am That I am*. What is I am but a declaration of our Beingness. The natural rhythm of breath becomes the steady joy of Beingness - breath is pure Beingness - and our Beingness is our Source.

If thou art a true seeker, thou shalt at once see Me: thou shalt meet Me in a moment of time. Kabir says, "O Sadhu! God is the breath of all breath."
  -Kabir Sahib

3) Sense withdrawal (Pratyahara)

Meditation shuts out the outer world to bring focus to the inner world - this is the beginning of meditation. Our inner world is connected to the outer world and therefore is equally as important, if not more.

Closing your eyes, bring your awareness to your inner world - this is where Consciousness resides, and Source speaks. The experience of sense withdrawal is comparable to falling into a deep sleep on the couch after a hard day at work only to awaken to family or friends busy around you making sounds that you had blocked out. That sensation of shutting out the outer world because the focus is so strong on the inner world is Pratyaharah.

4) Creating a Point of Focus

Place your gaze slightly above the middle of your eyebrows; not on the skin, but outwards a little. Create a white dot, or white light, like a diamond, or a blue dot, or a blue gem in your imagination, whichever you feel calls you, and make this the point of focus. If this is hard to locate or focus on, it can be helpful to briefly place your finger on the skin, slightly above the middle of your eyebrows, to help anchor the location.

Make this the point of focus. As thoughts come and go, it can be helpful to imagine them being pulled into the dot, helping you bring your focus back.

Overtime, with continued practice, you will develop the feeling of the location of the mystical third eye in your brain, called *Ajna,* in Sanskrit. To focus on this region truly does quiet the mind and open the space for our Consciousness.

The Proclamations

As long as I have been teaching meditation, when one begins speaking a word, rhythmically with their breath, focusing becomes easier. I rely on an ancient Vedic system, as I was taught by my teacher, called Proclamation Meditation, the goal of which is to meditate on statements of your identity which proclaim your relationship to the Universe. In Sanskrit, they are called *Mahavakyam* meaning 'great words,' and originate from the 8th century sage Shankara, who developed them as a way of distilling the essence of the Vedas into concise statements of power, capturing the quantum unified field, Brahman, in all its glory.

In Ancient Times when the student or the neophyte came to the Master, he was told the meaning of one Proclamation at a time. Then the Master told him to continuously repeat the Proclamation till the Master felt the student had internalized it. The student became the Proclamation...Each Proclamation leads to the next in perfect harmony in order for the student to attain the realization that he and the Universe are One, not two.
   -Tulshi Sen: Ancient Secrets of Success for Today's World

Consciousness is beyond the mind, and the Mahavakya are designed to penetrate through its limitations of past, present, and future. The power associated with saying these words will open the doors to a greater experience of Consciousness, as I have seen over many years of teaching this meditation. And their potential, when merged with your identity, will have you experiencing your Higher Self, and becoming the designer of your life.

As we move towards the Rising, we will continue on the path of Mahavakyam Meditation, introducing a new Mahavakyam where appropriate. Each proclamation originates from a verse in the Vedas, which will be provided.

The First Proclamation

Begin your Proclamation meditation by repeating the first proclamation; **Pragyanaam Brahman** (Source: Rg Veda, Aitareya Upanishad 3.3).

Phonetically it is;

Pra-gya-naam Bra-hma

Pragyanaam means Consciousness, but its specific translation is; prior to naming - the place of Consciousness before the forms of thought are created. This is the Absolute, the source of Consciousness.

Brahman is the conscious unified field.

Pragyanaam Brahman translated from Sanskrit is therefore <u>Consciousness is the Creator</u>.

Pragyanaam Brahman denotes an awareness of Consciousness; that we are Consciousness, and Consciousness is all things. The Universe, Brahman, is unlimited by substance, producing substance out of itself, therefore all things are made with and by Consciousness.

Repeat this Proclamation in your meditation by breathing in through your nose and on your exhale, say Pra-gya-naam Brah-ma by elongating the vowels; not too fast and not too slow.

5) Concentration and Higher States of Consciousness

The next step of meditation is the ebb and flow of prolonged culmination of concentration. Concentration feels good because you put aside your thinking for pure focus - you get your mind out of the way. In life, whatever the activity, it is concentration that makes one excel.

It is concentration that quiets the mind to attain a pure moment experience. It is also concentration that allows one to experience the subtle feelings and sensations of intuition, opening us to realms unknown. That which is unknown to us becomes known through concentration.

Awareness and concentration are akin to sunlight and a magnifying glass; sunlight will spread out over an area evenly, but when a magnifying glass is used to focus, its power intensifies, enough to cause a fire.

Here is a guide on the culmination of concentration to help you, as broken down by the sage Patanjali;

Dharana - is the singular act of grabbing onto your object of focus.

Dhyana - is the continuous concentration on your object of focus.

Dharana and *Dhyana* are different, each carrying a distinct feeling. For example, focus on any object you see in your environment; that is *Dharana*. When continuous concentration has quieted your mind, that is *Dhyana*. The distinction is *Dhyana* is the continuous flow of cognition, the feeling of holding the one-pointed focus, like a stream of water - constant and continuous.

Samadhi - the desired state, is the experience of Unity in meditation and should flow naturally from deep *Dhyana*. *Samadhi* is a door opened, a light revealed, a curtain peeled back. It can only be experienced and not spoken of. *Samadhi* is like the calm of the ocean when there are no waves. It is multi-dimensional expressed as Light seen. In Sanskrit, *Samadhi* means 'becoming the same,' that is becoming One, into Unity. The clarity of mind from deep concentration becomes an experience of serenity - serenity leads to Unity.

On an undisturbed mind...the concentration on subtle sense perceptions can cause steadiness of mind.
Or by concentration on the supreme, ever-blissful Light within.
Or by concentrating on a great soul's mind which is totally freed from attachment to sense objects.
Or by concentrating on an experience had during dream or deep sleep.
Or by meditating on anything one chooses that is elevating.
Gradually, one's mastery in concentration extends from the primal atom to the greatest magnitude.
The Yoga Sutras of Patanjali - Verses 35-40

Summary

Try the above five steps in either a single session, or if meditation is new to you and they appear overwhelming, break them up and give yourself time to get used to them.

You can start by focusing on the rhythm of your breath with *Hamsa*. Then when you are ready, bring your focus to a concentrated dot on the third eye.

Then when you feel comfortable you can combine the five steps using the following summary.

1) Find a comfortable position to sit, having a straight but not strained back - half lotus position is an option.
2) Breathe into your belly naturally, through the nose, noticing the pause in between the expansion and contraction of the diaphragm.
3) Close your eyes and bring your awareness inward.
4) Choose an object of focus; dot in the third eye, and either *Hamsa* with the rhythm of your breath, or a Proclamation out loud.
5) Notice the movements from *Dharana, Dhyana,* and *Samadhi*.

...first of all, you must understand the meaning of meditation. Real meditation is a state completely free of thoughts. This is how the great sage Maharishi Patanjali defined meditation in his Yoga Sutras: yogashchitta vritti nirodhah, "Yoga is to still the movements of the mind."
...Meditation should happen very naturally. It should be completely spontaneous. This space that you attain when the prana goes out and dissolves and when the apana comes in and dissolves, this space where there is no thought, no object, is true meditation. It is natural meditation, the highest meditation.
   -Swami Muktananda; I am That

Creating a Regular Habit of Meditation

The best way to sustain a regular habit of meditation is by creating a space in which it can be regularly practiced; maybe a small corner in your bedroom, or in another room where you won't be disturbed. Try using a comfortable pillow and decorate the area with objects or pictures that have meaning for you. If you can, meditate once in the morning, and once in the evening, each for five to ten minutes.

Using a mala that is imbued with power, I move a bead through my fingers for every breath, called *japa* in Sanskrit, which results in 108 breaths for every meditation, typically lasting 10-15 minutes depending on the length of the breaths. You can do the same, or you can count your breaths on your fingers, or you can use a timer for 5 or 10 minutes, or you can use none of the above and end your meditation when you feel ready. Do what is comfortable.

Meditating before bed is great for treating insomnia. While getting my master's degree, I conducted a meditation class at the university to help students and teachers handle stress.

One day, a fellow master's student who was taking my class, chatting with me afterwards, commented, "We are not getting any sleep. I know a lot of us students, all we do in bed is think about all the work we have to do. Wouldn't you agree?"

Blankly, I said, "No."

I could not relate as I didn't have a problem sleeping and felt a little awkward, but I sympathized with him. I never gave it too much thought exactly why I was sleeping, and my fellow students were not, especially in the stressful times of doing our master's. Then one day in meditation class, my fellow student heard that I meditate before I retire to bed and realized that might be the difference between myself and others who weren't getting a proper night's sleep. Low and behold, he tried meditating before retiring for the night and afterwards when he laid down in bed, he fell asleep right away.

Meditating with the Distracted Mind

Often, I find new meditators hard on themselves when learning to meditate. We feel we must be amazing at something we start and if we are not, we don't want to do it, but we didn't learn to ride a bike by being a great bike rider first.

Your mind may wander, no problem, just bring it back. You may struggle with meditation, no problem just enjoy what you can in the moment; enjoy your breath, just observe. You may fall asleep, that's great, it means you're relaxing. That kind, gentle attitude is important during the learning process, as meditation is something we get better at over time. Importantly, we never want to create frustration in our meditation.

It's normal for our mind to wander in meditation. You may think of problems, ideas, or dreams - have compassion with yourself and just observe your thoughts. I have solved many work and home problems when my mind began to dwell on my issues while meditating, then by bringing my attention back to deep concentration, breath and the third eye, my subconscious instantly bursts forth an idea that solves the problem. Bringing my mind back to a point of focus gave my subconscious the space to figure out my issues - I got out of my own way.

As well, know that it is in the resistance that strength is made. For example, we build muscles in a workout by lifting a weight, but technically it is in the tension of the weight wanting to fall to the ground, and our resistance from letting it do so, that builds our muscle. The same with meditation; when your mind is all over the place, it is the act of bringing it back to a point of focus that creates mental strength.

Some find sitting still hard on their body. Over time it gets easier to handle the full length of your meditation. Again though, be kind to yourself and sit in a comfortable position so you are not thinking about your body.

When we're meditating, we may have unexpected experiences; emotions may come up, maybe a feeling of emptiness, or jealousy, or anger. It's OK. Try to be curious; why are you having these feelings? Observe yourself from the outside and just be aware of them.

You may feel tired, excited, annoyed, or even boredom - instead of reacting to your emotions automatically, watch them come and go. You may experience many different emotions in your meditation but do your best to observe them and continue to bring your awareness back to your breathing and object of focus.

Lastly, I like to offer a solution to handling the mind that I use in meditation. When my mind is trying to control and distract me, I offer up the problem to Source. For example, I'm thinking about the meal I will cook for dinner during my meditation. I then offer the making of the meal to Source by saying *Source will make that meal for me, I don't have to think about it right now*, or *Source will take care of it*. Let go of the need to control in the present moment by offering to Source the completion of the worry or the issue. Let Source take care of it for you. Importantly, you can think about it later.

Our Inner Architecture: Discerning the Voice of the Mind and the Voice of the Heart

Now that we have a practice of learning how to quiet the mind, how do we know what to listen to within ourselves amongst the different thoughts, tendencies, sensations, and impulses? Intuition is our inner teacher but how do we know when we are listening to it? When we have to make a choice in our lives, and all we have to go by is our feelings, how do we know what's right for us?

Simply put, our heart is our truth. Pure feeling in our heart is like an experience of energy inside us - an experience of pure Beinghood. How we feel about things is a great indication of what our truth is.

Yet our mind, which is created from the brain, is attached to our senses - eyes, ears, taste, touch, smell. It tells us who we think we are, constructed from our world around us, and what it thinks is real, based on what it has observed.

When I speak of our heart being our truth, I do not imply our emotions, which are still chemical impulses from our brain. Our emotions can be reactions to how we feel, but they are not how we feel. Feeling is the originator.

Now, your mind is not your brain, and your brain is not your mind. Your brain, though a tool for your use, creates chemical impulses creating your experience of emotions, which become impressions into your mind. This mind could be considered your spiritual mind, or ethereal mind. This very biological experience of brain can complicate, trick, fool or confuse your experience of your true identity as awareness, or spirit, here on Earth.
-The Mystic Book

The voice of the heart and the voice of the mind can be hard to distinguish within us, but they are easy to locate because they originate from different regions of our body. Their voices are distinctly different, and sometimes there can be a conflict between the two, which is why the classic Vedic scripture the Bhagavad Gita was a battle, symbolizing the everyday fight between the heart and the mind.

This discerning of the voices of the heart and mind is a lifelong learning process. One day, after asking my Master about his process of listening to his heart, he described to me that he commits to its voice all the time - all day, every day. And this was evidenced to me by his continuous spontaneity that revealed itself to be highly intuitive; sometimes changing the location of a Satsang, or its topic on the spot, only to find the new direction helped someone or provided healing.

What most of us do is hear from the heart once or twice about one truth or another, and then the mind runs off with it yelling it heard from the heart and now it understands and doesn't need to listen to it anymore.

The Story of Two Birds beautifully symbolizes the relationship between these two voices within us.

The Story of Two Birds
A Love Story of the Soul and of the Mind

This is the story of two birds, one that was living in a golden cage and the other who was living free in the forest. Somehow, by the wondrous work of the Almighty they met and fell in love.

It is a mystery what the Almighty had in Its mind.

The bird of the forest told the bird of the cage, "Come, let's fly away free to the forest together."

The bird of the cage said to the bird of the forest, "Come stay with me in the cage, it is comforting, secure and well protected."

The bird of the forest said, "No, I will not let myself be caged and shackled."

The bird of the cage replied, "How can I go to the forest? I can't."

So the bird of the forest sat outside the cage and sang the songs of freedom of the forest. The bird of the cage sat in its golden cage and sang the songs it had been taught to sing.

"Why don't you sing the songs of the forest, the songs of freedom?" asked the bird of the forest.

"Why don't you learn the songs of the cage?" replied the bird of the cage.

The bird of the forest said, "No, I don't want to sing taught songs. I don't want to sing songs you were made to sing. I want to sing the songs of my heart."

"How can I sing songs of the forest?" asked the bird of the cage.

The bird of the forest said, "Look up at the open sky, absolutely clear blue. There are no limits anywhere.

The bird of the cage responded, "Look at this golden cage; it is furnished, neat and tidy and secure."

The bird of the forest sighed, "Let go of yourself. Release yourself amidst the clouds and spread your wings and fly with me and feel the freedom."

The bird of the cage heaved, "I am in this place of comfort, luxury and well protected where there is no trouble. Come, live with me, and enjoy the security and all the comforts that go with it."

"No, I cannot live in your golden cage. There is nowhere to fly," said the bird of the forest.

The bird of the cage replied, "How can I go with you to the clouds? There is nowhere to sit on the clouds."

This is a tale of two birds that fell in love with each other but could not reconcile their feelings. They were in love but could not be together. Between the rods of the cage, they touched each other's face. They looked at each other's eyes. But one could not understand the other or convince the other of the freedom of the forest or the luxury of the cage.

They stayed alone in their own worlds and hit their wings against the cage to feel each other and to love. And with great pain, the bird of the cage, hitting its wings against the cage asked, "Come closer."

The bird of the forest, full of agony replied, "No, if I come closer the cage door might close and I won't ever be free again."

The bird of the cage with a heavy submissive sigh said, "I don't have the strength to fly."

Translation in prose form by Tulshi Sen in Ancient Secrets of Success for Today's World of Rabindranath Tagore's Bengali poem Two Birds

In the first chapter we used the metaphor of the chariot, taken from the Vedic text the Katha Upanishad to describe our "inner architecture," that is, our relationship between mind and Consciousness. So, let's break down this description here.

Heart is Consciousness

As stated earlier, by referring to the heart we are not referring to emotions, which are produced from chemical processes in the brain, and are experienced in the heart region. Emotion is the mental choice we make in response to external or internal stimulus. This confusion between emotion and feeling is why it is important for us to learn to distinguish what is truly our truth.

By Consciousness we are referring to our awareness, which is experienced as our imagination, or the "imager" within, the thinker (thoughts are processed by the visual center in the brain, meaning all thoughts are images, which most people don't realize). Thoughts are produced out of our Being.

Our Consciousness, the imager within, is the part of us connected to no space and not time, which is the seat of our intuition, and the place in which we build Visions to manifest – this is pure feeling, and pure Being. This is our soul, this is Consciousness, and it knows your unlimited identity, and its foundation is the heart,

So, what is true for you? Look to your pure unobstructed feeling in the present moment.

The Brain is a Repository of Past Information

The human brain is like a computer, loading up information about its world from the five senses, assessing, and then making choices. And it can act like an animal of Earth when it relies on the senses; caring about its own needs, looking out for its survival, and scared for the future.

The mind is the residual energy of the physical brain and has a greater potential than we humans are presently using. While our spirits are not of earth, having a greater capacity than we can comprehend. The mind often tries to limit our spirit in line with its own understanding by using the brain.

I am not talking negatively about the mind or the brain, as we need them to conduct our everyday tasks, but they act as a filter of Consciousness; filtering out what it can't understand based on past information and replacing it with what it does understand.

Your present state of mind tries to interpret and translate the message (of Consciousness) in accordance with the tendencies of the mind.
   -Tulshi Sen; Ancient Secrets of Success for Today's World

Meditation brings awareness to this relationship of mind and Consciousness. There is no reading to help you understand this; there is intellectual guidance, but it is only through experience can you know that Consciousness is the foundation of the mind.

Consciousness is behind the Mind and the foundation of the Mind. Consciousness is the reality and the Creator of your world. Mind is the processor....Both Mind and Body are restricted to time and space. Consciousness is not trapped in time and space. Consciousness is free from past, present, and the future. It is Unity…The Mind is the instrument and the Seer is your Consciousness, like the binoculars are the instrument and You are the Seer. Mind is not Consciousness.
   -Tulshi Sen; Ancient Secrets of Success for Today's World

Consciousness is the imager/thinker, while the mind is like an interpreter along for the ride with us, providing its own filter or taking control all together. It is the tool with which we use to concentrate awareness, focusing Consciousness to create the world around us, directing it where we choose to create reality.

It can be helpful to think of thoughts as something we tune into from our Being, with Consciousness simply responding to the limits we place on it from the beliefs the mind has gathered from the five senses. Which is why when we expand our idea of Consciousness to include our dimensional capabilities we begin to tune into other thoughts that include that awareness – you expand your mind and Consciousness responds.

The Intellect

The intellect is the chooser, choosing between mind and heart, between unconditioned present experience or past information. Do we listen to our heart and what it knows in pure feeling and Being, or do we listen to our mind and its interpretation of what it's been told about the world.

Which one should it listen to at any given moment?

Think about how your mind handles the past and future versus the heart. The mind predicts the future based on how you have lived out your past, while the heart may feel assured of a future with which your mind doesn't believe is possible.

Think about a choice you had to make recently, did you make the choice from your heart or from your mind.

List your last three major decisions.

1

2.

3.

Now was decision 1 made from the heart or mind?
_____

How about decision 2?
_____

How about decision 3?
_____

What were the outcomes of each?
Outcome 1

Outcome 2

Outcome 3

What did you learn from this analysis?

_____
_____
_____
_____

The deep secret here is that the heart knows it is Consciousness, knows it is connected to Source. It is the mind that holds its own identity of us, based on past experience.

What is Ego?

Ego is when we identify with our body, as a separate identity, not in Unity. When we identify as a Being in Unity then that is not ego. Therefore, to be egotistical is to engage in root thoughts and actions meant to self-preservate the state of ourselves as a separate identity from the world around us.

Again, this is not to create judgment because as the above definition implies, we will have an ego for our entire physical existence. It's more about observing the mind's tendency to create thoughts, words, and actions that root in a belief that we are not in Unity.

Discerning the Voices of the Heart and Mind Through Intentions of Love and Fear

Every thought imagined, every word uttered, and every action taken has an intention. Intentions are the originating impulse of our Consciousness into the physical world. All intentions can be taken to either be an intention of love or an intention of fear, plain and simple. If you think about this, you will know it to be true.

Now here is the connection; intentions of fear will be made from our mind, of past information or data from only what we know. While intentions of love are our Consciousness, our truth, and of the heart, and are made of current information, which could include past information but will be rounded out by our intuition or what we are truly feeling.

It's important here to clarify the difference between information and intention. Information is our learned knowledge of things with which we execute to function properly in society, such as; how to drive, conduct our jobs, and cook for our families. But the intentions of our actions, of our words, and of our thoughts matter, as they govern how we expect the world around us to respond. Plain and simple; if we are choosing our desires and actions from our minds then we are choosing an intention of fear, and if we are choosing intentions from love, we are coming from our heart, we are coming from Consciousness.

Take any thought you have and think about its intention. Can you discern if it is produced from an intention of love or fear? Even seemingly mundane thoughts root themselves in an intention of love or fear. For example, you are thinking about what's to eat in the fridge; eating can be comforting and provide nighttime enjoyment, so it can be an intention of love, love of self, but if you're using it to subside your mind from anxiety because of, say, tomorrow's workday, then it is an intention of fear. An intention of fear will have a feal; visceral, heavy, maybe darker, or may drain you. Intentions of love will be uplifting, lighter, feel good, may be energizing, or make you feel alive.

Learning to discern how fear and love manifest in the body is a great way of knowing if the intention of a thought, word, or action is our truth.

Try this exercise designed to open your awareness to the intentions of love and fear.

What does fear feel like to you? What images or associations come to mind?

For example, fear feels;
Heavy
Wants to grab
Feels sticky

Fill in your own.

_____
_____
_____
_____

What does love feel like to you? What images or associations come to mind?

For example, love feels;
Light
Lets go
Feels clean

Fill in your own;

_____
_____
_____
_____

With the above exercise in mind, can you identify the intention of something you thought today?

Thought had: _____

Was it an intention of love or fear? _____

Can you identify the intention of something you said out loud to someone today?

Thing said: _____

Was it an intention of love or fear? _____

Can you identify the intention of something you did today?

Action taken: _____

Was it an intention of love or fear? _____

What did you learn from this exercise?
_____
_____
_____

Being State

Being state can be hard to conceive because we are constantly in a state of doing to accomplish the activities in our lives. We go to work, make a phone call, drive to the mall, mail a letter, send off emails - we are constantly in a state of Doing. This is a state of mind that supports an autopilot-like experience.

To fully live from Consciousness we live from what we choose to Be, that is, what we choose as our Beingness while we Do. In our world we are trained to think that if we want to Be something we have to Do something, but this creative act tells us we need to Be something, then we Do. It is a fundamental paradigm shift to change from "Doing to Being," to "Being to Doing." Living from our Being state does not mean we do not Do, it simply means we choose what we want to Be while we Do. Choosing a Being state helps us to take control of our lives by choosing how we want to experience what we are experiencing; in essence we are choosing the experience. By following this, your life will change, and the conscious Universe will respond, guaranteed.

To understand Being state we need to learn to, well...just sit with yourself and Be – just exist. Sometimes that is a hard place to get to because we are so used to Doing.

I encourage you right now to take a second and let yourself Be.

Now ask yourself what are you Being?

When we are just Being, we are not acting automatically or in a goal-oriented mode, but are conscious of our experience, and are connected to the present moment.

Now, let's think about what we are typically trying to Be while we Do the things we Do. For example, I like to go for an evening walk to Be healthy, or maybe to Be clear headed, i.e. grounded. I kiss my partner to Be connected, or to Be in love.

Try thinking about what you Do and what Beingness you are trying to achieve.

Write down some things that you Do?

_____
_____
_____
_____

Now what are you trying to Be while you Do what you Do?

_____
_____
_____
_____

Throughout our entire life we are constantly in the process of Being someone; a father, a mother, a friend, a good worker, a boss, a person who is happy, sad, or successful. We have taken the images around us to form our sense of who we should Be, which in turn defines the thoughts we produce, which then shape and create our experiences in the world. Our Being and thoughts about ourselves creates our idea of what is achievable in the world.

Living creatively is choosing who we want to Be first, before we approach the events of our lives. Literally, who do you think you are? Who are you desiring to Be? What type of person do you think you are?

Right now, pick up your cell phone and find an event in the news. Try to find an event you don't consider yourself an expert on, or haven't formulated a lot of thoughts about. Read enough to just get an idea of what is being said.

Now ask yourself: who am I in response to this event? Who do I want to Be in relation to this event? What type of person do I want to Be?

What was your response to these questions?

Choosing an authentic response, and not from the images you have gathered from those around you - from how you think you should respond, or what your parents, society, or authority figures think - is intrinsic and produces happiness.

Sometimes, when things get hectic, I have to remember to ask myself, *who do I want to Be in this moment?* We can respond very automatically to the event's in our lives, yet asking who you want to Be in the moment, and acting on it, makes our response conscious.

Being state is our engine of creation, so we will explore it again in the chapter *We Are Creator Beings With the Power to Create Reality Through Visioning.*

Vigilance Regarding Our Mind, the Filter of Our Consciousness

To come to our Consciousness purely, we need to be vigilant about our minds' role in constantly filtering our experience of life. Ideally this is the purpose of a meditation practice, or any practice one uses to wholly come to Consciousness.

The Masters say that just because your Consciousness has been awakened it does not mean a thing if you don't have control over your mind. All limitation is of the mind and all freedom is of the mind...Your Consciousness is not your mind. It is the urge in you to experience Bliss which transcends happiness. You get glimpses of it in moments of your life. These moments become frozen in your mind. Moments like when you hold your baby for the first time in your arms or when you are engulfed in a romantic embrace or when you get immersed in the glory of a sunrise against the mountains....Consciousness is behind the Mind and the foundation of the Mind. Consciousness is the reality and the Creator of your world. Mind is the processor.
 -Tulshi Sen; Ancient Secrets of Success for Today's World

The method to gain vigilancy over our minds' role in filtering our lives is to have as pure of an experience of Consciousness as possible, that is to have experiences of God, Unity, or Universal Source in our heart, which we will expand on throughout this book. As well, Visioning and manifesting the Vision (which we talk about a little later) provides awareness on our minds tendencies to take control of the desires of our heart. Experiencing both Source and Visioning will provide for you the marked difference between mind and heart, and awareness how our mind creates its forms, filtering Consciousness.

The goal is to know and master the mind, the filter of our Consciousness, which leads us to our next section - The Ocean of the Mind.

The Ocean of the Mind

The mind, our greatest personal tool, focuses on the outside world, pretending spirit doesn't exist, and therefore never knowing the magical inner forces and power that can support us in our daily life. Therefore, to make the mind work for our spirit we have to understand it and control it. The less stress and extreme emotion we experience in daily life, the greater our inner resources to listen to our spirit, which we can tap into as a source of personal power.

Also, it's the hardware we use to perceive and create our world, literally. When our mind is rocky, our life is rocky. When our mind is at peace, our life is at peace.

"As the mind, so the person; bondage or liberation are in your own mind. If you feel bound, you are bound. If you feel liberated, you are liberated. Things outside neither bind or liberate you; only your attitude toward them does that.

So, if you can have control over the thought forms and change them as you want, you are not bound by the outside world. There's nothing wrong with the world. You can make it a heaven or hell according to your approach.
-Swami Satchidananda; Commentaries to The Yoga Sutras of Patanjali*

In this section we unravel the "why" behind our mind, to understand its tendencies and thinking, expand our awareness, and choose thoughts that ground, empower, and prepare us to receive our spirit for our Rising. The tendencies that shape our thinking are born in the subconscious. So, we start our journey by understanding its language - the language of our own inner symbology.

The Symbolic Self

Deep within each of us is a subconscious mind that lies close to our pure unobstructed Consciousness, interpreting its impulses, and rectifying the differences between both its and the minds desires, and translating them in meaningful ways with which we can learn to interpret, understand, and fulfill.

In essence there are two "personalities" within each of us; one that is logical, looks for definitions, explanations, and concrete circumstances (the mind), and the other with which derives wisdom from events, sees them symbolically, and interprets deeper meaning than our logical mind sees (the subconscious). This 'other' self is immersed in symbolism - thus it is our 'symbolic self,' and its language is that of God and the soul - the language of symbols, images, stories, myths, and metaphors.

What is a symbol? A symbol is such when its meaning is larger than what is implied, containing an unconscious side, and it may inspire ideas beyond the logical mind.

Symbols even produce spiritual experiences when meditated upon such as with mandalas or yantras in Hindu philosophy. Our symbolic self also speaks through parables, metaphors, stories, and myths, as every dream is a story, and every Vision or desire is part of our personal mythos. Think about your favorite movie and its plot. It is loved by your subconscious, for the story it tells about itself.

This is the reason the artist is one who is spiritual, for their act of turning their inner symbols into an outward expression. The highest joy of the successful artist is to communicate the collective Consciousness as an individual expression, to produce something that lives into the next step of human evolution.

Our evolution towards our Source is an embrace of the symbolic self which sits close to our spirit. The easiest way to come to this symbolic self is by being observant of the symbols in our dreams, and with active imagination, and pareidolia. By doing so, we begin to expose the subtle impulses of our thoughts, bring to life our deep feelings, our personal symbology, and we acquire the skill set of listening to our pure intuition, uninhibited by the mind.

So, it starts with dreams, and your personal dream symbology, the true interpretation of which can only be done by you.

For this exercise it requires a dream that you have recorded.

Recording Your Dreams

Either have a journal and a pen beside your bed to write down your dream or use a smartphone to audio record your voice describing it. If you choose to write down your dream, try using paper and pen and not be tempted to write notes in a smartphone, as its light impacts your ability to concentrate on the details of the dream.

Before you get up for the day, while still in bed, record as much detail as you can possibly remember of your dream. It's important to not leave your bed while recording as the position you slept in can help with recalling more details. If something is unclear, or you only remember part of the sequence of events of the dream, no problem, just record as many details as you can.

Learning From Your Dream

After you have recorded your dream, later in the day, with a clear mind, come back to either your dream journal, or the audio recording.

Rewrite here the content, detail, and feelings in your dream. Write as much detail as you can.

_____
_____
_____
_____

Even if our dreams are confusing or convoluted, try approaching them with an assumption that somehow they make sense. To do that, focus on the feelings that were in the dream.

What is similar in this dream to your life right now?

Where is the feeling similar in your everyday waking life?

The symbols in the dreams are all aspects of yourself, therefore what are those parts of your self telling you?

Choosing one object or idea presented in your dream, ask why this symbol and not a different one? For example, why a broom, instead of a stick?

What do you think is the underlying intent of your dream?

If you lived out your dream in reality, what would you change?

If you were to dance, paint, or write a song about your dream, what would it look like? What other symbols does it inspire?

What would be the title of this dream?

List all of the symbols of your dream. This would be all the objects, including details of the environment. Record all the symbols first, then write what you think is the meaning or each. Don't think about it too much if you don't know, just write off the top of your head what you think it could mean.

Symbol : _____
Meaning:_____

Symbol : _____
Meaning:_____

Symbol : _____
Meaning:_____

Symbol : _____
Meaning:_____

Symbol : _____
Meaning:_____

Symbol : _____
Meaning:_____

Symbol : _____
Meaning:_____

Symbol : _____
Meaning:_____

Symbol : _____
Meaning:_____

Symbol : _____
Meaning:_____

What did you learn about your subconsciousness's inner symbology? What stuck out to you?

_____

_____

If you continue to practice recording your dreams and analyzing them, you will increase your ability to recall their symbols and the sequence of events in fuller detail. And by repeatedly studying your dreams, over time you will become familiar with the symbols that your subconscious repeatedly uses, and their meaning to you.

You can also use dreams to help you with solving problems in waking life. If you're facing a challenge, before you go to bed, close your eyes and ask your dream to provide clarity to your problem and see what it produces.

Active Imagination

Carl Jung is credited for being the first to accept play as a form of psychotherapy, through what he called 'active imagination,' as a method of retrieving the impulses and messages of the unconscious. How he learned the value of active imagination comes from an interesting story of his.

One day, after feeling he couldn't understand the source of a disturbance in his psyche, he decided to open himself up to the images and impulses of his unconscious mind and do whatever it suggested to him. He began gathering stones by a lakeside and making a village, all from the impulse of what he felt was in his unconscious. He found himself living out his childhood games. He was building a town with rocks and sticks, even reluctantly, to access the deep images and impulse that was guiding him. Now this is in 1913, a husband, doctor, father, university professor, and here he was feeling humiliated, in his mind acting like a child. With childlike manner he built a full town of stone and mud, including gates and arches, cottages, and a castle. He realized it was missing the church. While looking for the material to build the church he found a perfectly cut pyramid along the beach to be used as the altar. When he placed the pyramid at the altar, he remembered a vivid dream that haunted him for years as a child which as an adult he had forgotten. A dream as a child he thought was about the underworld and ritual. He believed this to be a synchronicity. Through the process of play he was led to a deep-seated dream, and he felt this to be the cause of his disturbance. He recognized this childhood dream as his shadow, or the dark side of his unconscious. He spent a lot of time at that point bringing to light this dark dream and its meaning to his psyche. He called it "an initiation into the realm of darkness." As he continued imaginative play, his thoughts became clear and his emotional feelings were released. He seemed as best as he could to give the impulses, images, and dreams form, through creative play, drawings and paintings. By initiating in play Jung activated the imagination of his psyche which put him in touch with himself.

Active imagination is considered a dialogue with different parts of oneself, as a method to pursue the inner images and meaning of our life as seen from our unconscious.

Discovering Active Imagination

Active imagination has two parts.

First, it starts with a piece of content from your subconscious - a mood, an inner voice, a vision, a piece of a fantasy, or a dream image, such as one you recorded above, or even an emotion in your body.

Briefly describe here what your choosing:
_____
_____
_____

Second, select a form or mode of expression. It can be through modeling, drawing, painting, dancing, through drama, spoken out, visual, or through music.

Then let the emotions of this choice of inner object come to the conscious mind and be a point of departure for your choice of expression. Allow yourself to flow from the first impulse before your conscious mind can think about it - seek to express and create, and not analyze what you're creating. Continue to be as conscious of the emotions as possible as you express, giving yourself free rein to create whatever form comes through. Sink into the feeling without reserve and make note here of all the images, fantasies, and associations that come up.

_____
_____
_____
_____
_____
_____

As the unconscious content is taking form, come to it with an open mind and with curiosity how it has meaning. Have the idea of being a scientific observer of your psychic content and seek to understand it.

When you have become familiar with this exercise, try using only your imagination; see yourself expressing the inner content (vision, dream, fantasy) by using any means you desire in your imagination. You could imagine yourself singing your dream symbology or dancing your vision. See what feelings, images, or associations come up for you when you do this.

Pareidolia

When we are familiar with ushering the impulses and desires of the unconscious mind to the conscious mind through active imagination, we can then apply the same non-judgmental curiosity, and uncensorship to listening to our symbolic self daily by relying on pareidolia.

Pareidolia is finding meaningful visual patterns in what would otherwise be considered random or unrelated objects in your waking world. Maybe you can remember a time as a child when you stared at the clouds, letting your mind come up with images from the formless patterns, and seeing a hippopotamus or an old man's face.

When pareidolia is used as a method of bringing the impulses and desires of the unconscious to the conscious mind we may see symbols of our unconscious in everyday objects in the world around us. Maybe a group of trees looks like people hugging and your unconscious is feeling the need to be close to others. Maybe in a flock of birds you saw the pattern of stairs and you feel you're moving up in life.

Before trying to experience pareidolia, first bring to mind your subconscious, your symbolic self, by remembering a dream, or a time where active imagination successfully exposed your unconscious mind's images. Remember that feeling.

Another method, in case the above is too complicated, or it doesn't work for you, is simply feel and come from your heart. Whatever works.

Now, with that connection in mind look around your environment, and try to observe any meaningful patterns or images. Let your unconscious speak through your environment. What did you observe?

_____
_____
_____

What feelings were associated with the patterns or images?

_____
_____
_____

What did you feel it said about your unconscious?

_____
_____
_____

Seeing patterns in the waking world is a way for the conscious mind to listen to the always active unconscious mind, to merge both into one.

If this didn't work, no problem, try it again the next time you're out in nature and see if its abundant patterns help you experience pareidolia.

If after that you still found it difficult, no problem, we will come back to these exercises of the symbolic self in the following chapters. Applying a different modality might make it easier to experience pareidolia.

Using Impulses of the Unconscious as a Means to the Source

After my fifth contact event with the Elder in May of 1997, I began exploring Carl Jung's concept of active imagination by exercising play inside my mind, using only the imagery of my imagination. This inner play took upon the nature of creating shapes, orbs, and lights that I placed in my environment and moved around and interacted with. This mimicked (unbeknownst to me at the time) what I experienced on the craft when I moved crystalline objects with my mind, and also the orb exercises in the Mystic Book.

I started by connecting with a dream image, vision that I had, or simply a feeling within, and then using my imagination, I would let it create whatever shapes, lights, or forms it wanted.

Acting on the urges of the unconscious through active imagination began a process of learning to let my unconscious speak its content without the influence of my analytical mind. I soon found that when I orientated myself on the feelings in my heart, and then followed this practice, I was letting go to the urges of pure Consciousness - my soul. I discovered this was my intuitive self that had knowledge that did not come from my five senses, which could be about the environment, the people around me, or the future. This technique would help me in desperate moments while traveling, as told in *The Rising*, such as when I was in Quebec and my car broke down in the cold, urgently requiring me to seek help. I calmed myself, centered myself in my heart, and let my subconscious guide me with an arrow that led to saftey.

I reasoned that the unconscious was the interpreter of my soul, but not the soul, meaning I could get my intuition wrong if I wasn't working hard at keeping my conscious mind from distorting that first impulse. Therefore I learned to have a relationship with my unconscious mind and let its images be my intuitions language.

In summary, delve into your dream symbology, and live with active imagination and pareidolia as a means of pursuing the impulses of your unconscious, all as an act of moving closer to your Source.

The Power of the Present

The Entrapment of the Past and Future

The present moment is the only moment we have, and yet our brains have a tendency to obstruct it by dwelling on the past and future, with so many sounds, sents, sights, and sensations by-passing our awareness in any environment.

We can only be aware of Source in our lives by being present; Consciousness communicates only in the present, feeling only occurs in the present, and when your in love, you are not in love in the future or in the past, you are in love in the present, in the Now.

One of the greatest challenges of the mind is to not think about the past or the future.

If you are depressed, you are living in the past. If you are anxious, you are living in the future. If you are at peace, you are living in the present.
  - *Anonmous*

If we follow what we are told from quantum physics, then the past and future truly are constructs of the mind and are not of the real, therefore we waste away our experience of the Now by our conditioned reliance on them. This doesn't mean we don't make plans about our future, such as having a Vision or setting goals, or remember something we learned in the past to help us in the present. We simply want to be aware of our compulsion to be absorbed in the past or future, which takes us away from our experience of our Source.

Try right now to just close your eyes and watch your mind wonder. Notice how quickly it thinks about either the past or the future.

While conducting mindfulness workshops, I often get participants to do an exercise; I get everyone to tell me something they enjoy doing, such as a hobby, and then, once everyone has spoken, I ask them what is the similarity between everyone's responses. I give them a moment to think it over before I interject. The similarity is that each of our hobbies makes us present - we love to escape our thinking and be immersed in the present.

We want to cultivate our awareness to focus on the present moment at will, and this is because it helps us maintain a calm, and focused attention. It is our focus on the present moment in which we can observe if we are tense, stressed, frustrated, or angry, or if our energy is drained, or placed in the wrong direction.

For example, say you were laid off from your employment and you're renting an apartment. Now you don't know how you're going to pay next month's rent. Well, right now in the present, this month, rent is paid. Absorbing yourself in the present, not thinking of the future, will relax you and make you aware of your feelings, calmly. Then, you may have a feeling to call someone that could help you, that you weren't inclined to, or you may have a compulsion to go somewhere and network, when initially all your mind wanted to do was panic.

The Amazement and Wonder of the Now

One of the easiest ways to practice being in the present is with 'beginner's mind.' A beginner's mind is looking at something with new eyes and letting go of our ideas, perceptions, and concepts about it.

Our ability to see and connect with Source is linked to letting go of our ideas about what we are experiencing, including what we are seeing, hearing, smelling, tasting, and feeling, and just exist in the experience, wholly.

I remember as a child how I was enamored with the world; with the wonder, grandness, and the mystery of seeing things brand new. Maybe you have a child, know a child, or can remember being a child; how you saw the world around you new and fresh. With beginners mind we turn the natural wonder we had as children on to our seemingly mundane approach to our current world; the way a tree colours itself in fall, watching the wind blow and pick up the objects it interacts with, the play of shadows on the clouds during a sunset. The beginner's mind is excited and awed by simple things.

Look at a single object in your environment. Take a moment to ponder what it would be like to see this object as a child, to see it for the first time. Take notice of the shape, curves, and colours.

Now, take a minute to slowly look around your environment and imagine you're seeing all the details for the first time, with the mind of a child

How does it feel to do this exercise? What did you notice?

_____

_____

_____

If you had trouble with this exercise, no problem, try doing something new; see a new place, take a new path, or have an adventure. In a new environment or activity, it can be easier to remind ourselves what a beginner's mind feels like.

Beginner's mind can be used in many different ways. For example, we all have tasks to do that we can frame as being boring, but we can also influence what we find boring, and learn to appreciate it. When we love something, we focus on its details, therefore you can trick your mind by focusing on the details to make yourself love something.

Try it out, on a task you find boring or mundane.

Let's say you find washing dishes a drag. While washing them, try and have a beginner's mind; slow yourself down and feel the temperature of the water, notice the pressure as you apply it to the dishes, smell the soap, hear the water as it changes tones going over different plates. With wonder, think how amazing it is that your meals come from farmers' fields to the grocery store, to your stove, and to your plate.

That act of observation and immersion can induce an experience of connection and love of the moment. There is so much to be aware of at any given time, regardless of how we think about it.

By changing how we perceive our world with beginners mind we exercise our ability to be creative. Creativity is linked to a part of the brain which holds our perspective or "frame" of the world, and by changing it we loosen what is called our 'psychological rigidity.'

By also holding ourselves close to our beginner's mind we become more curious about life. We may wonder why things are the way they are, with a curiosity about our world and our Selves which creates a space to hear something new and different from what we may think is familiar. By coming from beginner's mind, we make our cup empty so Source can fill it.

Observing our Thoughts

Each day our attention is taken by the activities in our lives, as we engage with our work, family, and friends, appearing like we are externally focused, yet privately we live in a world filled with thoughts, much of which are unconscious. According to the National Science Foundation, a human has anywhere between 12,000 to 60,000 thoughts a day. So, as events are happening around us, we respond with unconscious automatic thoughts that govern our behaviour.

Our ability to experience our greatest desire, and our path out of our pains, are both achieved through our thinking. Therefore, it starts with awareness of what we are thinking about and replacing it with the thoughts we want. Yet, the problem is our thinking is ingrained in years of habit that has gone unconscious. It's only by observing ourselves in the Now that we can witness how we use our thoughts. And what we will find is that for every moment of every day we take what we know from the past to define the present and use it to expect the future. We can't break free from our limitations by living this way. The answer is in learning how to think about what we desire to think about.

The Power of the Observer Self

To be effective at observer awareness, we gather together our neutral thinking. What does this mean? Neutral thinking has no judgment, and accepts what is, letting things be without thought. So, observer awareness means to observe purely with no thought or judgment about what we are observing.

Have you ever been so engrossed in thought, then walked by a mirror and observed yourself, only to realize how absorbed you were in your thinking? This is the observer self.

In neutrality there is no right and wrong, and there is no attachment. And when applied to our lives, we see how our mind builds its ideas from the label it places on our experiences. All of your problems are in your head and the means to overcoming them is by approaching our thoughts with a neutral stance. With an observer mentality we see the equilibrium between good and bad, and right and wrong, as ideas.

By coming to our observer self we make a quick connection to objective reality. In objective reality events don't have implied meaning, but only take on the meaning we choose. For example, you are looking for employment and have been rejected from three interviews. You are implied to make a general causation that you are not hireable, because the mind desires to imply meaning. But your objective self sees these as separate events, not implying a general concept about yourself.

Observer self allows us to not be swayed by our environment, living in an equilibrium in our mind, with detachment, which are the strongholds of living a life of Consciousness. Why do we want to do this? Because Source exists objectively, it just exists, with no thought about its existence. Your Consciousness sees your life objectively. By moving into pure observer self, I can feel my Being is left - pure Being.

What is really happening in this moment? How am I interpreting what is happening? What are my emotions right now? Can I label them? What is the intention of my thoughts? The answer to all of these is in the observer self. My observer self sees what I am attempting to do in the world with the same compassion I see in others.

Here is an exercise to expand our awareness of our observer self;

First, think of a synonym for the word 'neutral.' For example, non-judgmental, or objective.
Second, describe some part of your life, a task or activity you engage in throughout your days. For example, cooking for your spouse, or driving the kids to school.
Third, ponder what it would feel like if you were experiencing your choice of synonym while engaged in your task?

Here's an example;

Neutral synonym:
<u>Non-judgmental</u>

A task or activity I engage in regularly:
<u>Cooking for my spouse.</u>

How does it feel to experience this part of your life this way?
<u>Freeing, with a pure feeling of an offering of love.</u>

Try it yourself.

Neutral synonym:
_____

A task or activity I engage in regularly:
_____

How does it feel to experience this part of your life this way?

_____
_____

Neutral synonym:

_____

A task or activity I engage in regularly:

_____

How does it feel to experience this part of your life this way?

_____
_____

Neutral synonym:

_____

A task or activity I engage in regularly:

_____

How does it feel to experience this part of your life this way?

_____
_____

Stepping Back From Thoughts

In all the meditation and coaching work I have done for others, every one of them wanted to think less. Thoughts are powerful, and we are all aware that they can override us. In this workbook we are not trying to stop our thinking, as that doesn't work, but simply reduce their power over us by shifting our relationship with them. By using our observer self, we gain the ability to step back from our thoughts.

What is a thought? Think about what you think a thought is.

One of the rewards from teaching meditation was witnessing learners realize that most thoughts are images, which move through our mind unconsciously.

We also think in words. For example, we might say in our minds, "What made that sound downstairs?"

Therefore, thoughts can be images, words, or both.

In truth though, thoughts are much more complex than this. We live in an illusion that they are one off events, as if they are only produced by our mind in response to an external event, and that's it. Yet, thoughts are more like packets of information that hold historical details about the thing we are thinking about. For example, a friend calls you up to tell you they just bought a hot rod sports car. As they explain their exciting new purchase, the thought that briefly drifts through your mind contains an image of a stereotypical rebellious greaser in a leather jacket; the type of person you think would own a hot rod sports car. Attached to the thought may be the first time you witnessed someone who owned a hot rod sports car, and their rebellious nature. You then put those thoughts aside and congratulate them on their fun purchase.

In the case of the example, the interconnected thoughts regarding the rebellious nature of someone who purchases a hot rod car, becomes a narrative – a story. That story may be based on past information, interpretations, opinions, possibly yours but not necessarily, and it all may or may not even be real.

Thoughts therefore are images and words that constitute our stories.

Below, write down a belief or concept about yourself, such as; I'm kind, I'm a hard worker, or I'm a family orientated person.

_____

Close your eyes and see the thought you have about this concept. Now write down here all the detail of that thought; the images you see and the feelings you experience.

_____
_____
_____
_____
_____
_____

Now, looking at your description, ask why you are choosing these images and feelings to describe yourself?

_____
_____
_____

Can you see the narrative that surrounds a single thought? Now ask yourself where did this story come from? Write here whatever response comes to mind.

Is this story based on fact, or is it based on an opinion?

Does it come from yourself or someone else?

Is the story helpful to you in your life? Does it help you grow or make you happy?

Now, let's try this same exercise with a thought you had today. Close your eyes and try to recall a thought that came to your mind today. It could have been about anything, just something you can bring to mind. Now write down here all the detail of that thought; the images you saw and feelings you experienced.

Now, going through the same questions in the last exercise, ask yourself where did this story come from? Write here whatever response come to mind.

Is this story based on fact, or is it based on an opinion?
_____
_____

Does it come from yourself or someone else?
_____
_____

Is the story helpful to you in your life? Does it help you grow or make you happy?
_____
_____

Why would we want to discover our stories? Because our brains are on automatic, constantly judging and producing information about our surroundings, creating assumptions and expectations, that are not necessarily real, and could be harming our happiness. Also, our thoughts keep us from living in the present where our Source is, where our Being is, the place where our intuition could be guiding us to think differently.

We are not our thoughts, yet we spend our entire life thinking we are.

Here are some simple techniques to reduce the power of our thoughts and the stories they belong to.

Close your eyes and take a breath. Just feel your breath for a few seconds. Now see yourself on a field; see the grass, see the clouds, feel a slight warm breeze. Now look up and observe the detail of a cloud over top of the field. Notice the cloud slowly moving away, how light it is, how it has no weight, like you can walk right through it. Now imagine any thought, about any story of your life, is this cloud. Make it this cloud. See the lightness of the cloud that is your thought, that it has no weight, like you can walk right through it. And see the thought just drift slowly away. See it go. See your thought move on as clouds do, with no weight; it is what it is, just a thought. Now take a deep breath, come back, and open your eyes when you're ready.

If during this meditation you felt a release, or disconnection from the thought, you experienced the psychological term called 'diffusion' - you diffused yourself from the energy of the thought, from the story. You were not your thoughts in that moment - you were just you. You were your I am.

Another method to diffuse the power of a thought is by creating an imagination that makes you feel good, and simply interjecting it into your stream of thinking. Think of a place that provides you with serenity and peace; maybe it's a place in a forest, on a mountain, or on a field, or maybe it's a simple image of a flower, or even something personal.

Take a moment to think about what that image is for you and then write it down here.

_____

_____

When you're aware you're thinking about something you don't want to think about, see this image instead.

Another powerful tool which comes from my Guru's teachings is to laugh at your thoughts. *Laughter lightens* he would say. If you're having a fearful thought, say "Cock-a-doodle-do" to it. *Life is not meant to be serious*, he would say.

Don't wait to use these tools when times in life are stressful. We gain the skill sets to manage our thoughts when we practice while things are going well, then when stressful times do arise you will be equipped to handle them.

In summary, if your having negative thoughts, see them as clouds and disconnect from their story, or replace the thought with a pleasant or serene one, or laugh at your thought and say "Cock-a-doodle-do."

But what if these techniques still didn't work? Our emotions and thoughts can challenge us. How do we handle them?

Dealing with Difficult Thoughts

We all have difficult thoughts. Sometimes they have a center of gravity that steers our inner world; maybe it's blame, maybe it's envy, maybe it's something you're afraid to admit to yourself, and so it seems like your thoughts have a mind of their own. Whatever it is, it's hard to stop and let go. We have all been there.

When your thoughts are running amuck, try to take a step back from them. Have curiosity. Ask yourself why are you so challenged by this thought? What happens when you listen to your thought with empathy? What comes up for yourself? Sometimes asking the right questions to ourselves can unlock the underlying stories.

Reflect on how the difficult thought is affecting your body. What does it feel like? Can you describe it? What effect does the thought have on your emotions? Can you label the emotions?

What happens when you bring the emotion closer to you? Feel the emotion fully - accept the emotion. Breathe into the difficult thought and keep the sensations close to you, stay with them. Then what happens? What thoughts do you have? What comes to mind?

While taking psychology classes in undergrad, we would often hear about fight or flight in terms of how humans have evolved to handle stress. The example would often be placed in the context of a caveman seeing a saber tooth tiger and either running away out of fear or choosing to fight. This analogy seemed antiquated and unrelatable, and only in context to say, some kind of extreme danger such as being robbed, or being in an accident or disaster.

It wasn't till my work teaching meditation that I realized how accurate the fight or flight analogy was to our everyday experience. Thoughts, even seemingly mundane ones, take on a flight or fight characteristic. For example, your irritated by a coworker and you know you probably are going to have to talk to them about their behaviour; you either anticipate yourself getting angry and are arguing with them in your head (fight), or are uncomfortable with having to approach them and the stress therefore is in your body and your acting in a way to suppress your uncomfort through eating, drinking, or zoning out (flight).

When we are having difficult thoughts, it can be helpful to see them as a product of the rambling mind that has evolved to sense danger and is resorting to either fight or flight. Be on the lookout for thoughts that seek to fight, such as self-bullying, arguing with yourself, or even suppressing or forcing thoughts, and thoughts that seek to flight such as zoning out, numbing yourself, distracting, hiding, or escaping.

Another helpful method for dealing with difficult thoughts is 'dissociation,' which is labeling the thought as a product of your over rambling mind. Say to yourself, "My mind is having the thought that...(fill in the blank)". It's not you, but the mind that you own that is having the thought. In this way you stop identifying the thought as yours but instead a product of your brain.

Handling our Emotions

Emotions are a product of our brain, but place themselves in our body. Therefore, to bring greater awareness to our thoughts, it can be helpful to gain awareness of our emotions. As we approach our emotions try having an accepting, compassionate, yet curious attitude. Most importantly, we don't want to judge or have negative thoughts about our emotions.

Emotions have a location in the body in which they place themselves. Close your eyes and notice where you feel the emotion in your body. Just let it be without fighting it. Make space for it, and just observe it. Be curious about the emotions size, shape, and colour that it creates in your imagination.

Now how does it feel to breathe into and accept the emotion?

As you feel your emotion, be aware of what thoughts you want to have. What is your first impulse?

When we are on autopilot, we can sometimes be susceptible to negative thinking and internal dialogue such as "I can't do it," "Know one really cares about what I do," or "'I'm lazy." We can have these thoughts and dialogue without even noticing it, which will then create unhelpful emotions. Typically, all you notice is that you're tired or emotionally drained.

If you catch your self in this scenario, then you can apply the above exercises to release the emotions;

<u>Accept the emotion, hold it close and breathe into it, see the thoughts that arise when you do, and know your negative thinking or dialogue is a story, just like a cloud over a field.</u>

It is a wise modo to never run away from uncomfortable emotions within. When feeling an uncomfortable emotion, feel it with kindness, acceptance, and care as best as you can. Be open to the emotion within your body, move into it closely and notice where it takes shape and form. Breathe into it. Allow the emotion to be as it is, fully. By becoming aware of the emotion, you recognize you are not the emotion, but the observer of the emotion.

A Little Extra on Creating Room for Repressed Emotions

Dr. Elisabeth Kubler-Ross and David Kessler, in their book *On Grief and Grieving (2007)*, identify what they call our five natural emotions which are grief, anger, envy, fear, and love. When emotions are repressed, they become distorted and create other types of harmful or damaging emotions. We have all repressed our emotions, at times more so than others. How we react to our emotions is often based on childhood programming, so using their model I created a simple exercise to explore how we handle emotions, which can further open us up to our thought patterns.

Below is a description of the five natural emotions. As you read, simply be aware of how your body feels. If there is any tightness in your body, be present with an open, observing attitude, feel it fully, and breathe into it.

Here is an outline to help you create room for your emotions as you read.

1) Become aware of how the emotions feel in your body - feel it fully.
2) Unhook any thoughts you have about the emotion - just let it sit and accept it.
3) Close your eyes, feeling the sensation of the emotion in your body, and breathe into it - just observe whatever thoughts arise.

Underneath the description, write notes if you feel compelled, describing how it is that you deal with your emotions in this way. Be gentle with yourself.

Grief is the natural feeling of loss or sadness. It can be a large sense of loss for something meaningful or something small such as the loss of a favourite object. When expressed we move through the grief. When we repress it, it can become depression.

Anger is a natural emotion. It is the tool you have which allows you to say, "No, thank you." It does not have to be abusive, and it never should be damaging to another. When expressed, we move through anger. When repressed, it becomes rage.

Envy is a natural emotion. It is the emotion that makes you want to do something again, to try harder, to continue striving until you succeed. When expressed, we move through envy. Envy repressed becomes jealousy.

Fear is a natural emotion. All babies are born with only two fears: the fear of falling, and the fear of loud noises. All other fears are learned responses brought on by the environment and taught to the child by their parents. The purpose of natural fear is to build in a bit of caution to keep the body alive. When expressed, we move through fear. If repressed it becomes panic.

Love is a natural emotion. When it can be expressed, and received, normally and naturally, without limitation or condition, it does not require anything more. When expressed, we move through love. When repressed love becomes possessiveness.

What did you learn from this exercise? Can you label which emotions you typically repress? Did you bring to light any thought patterns that unconsciously affect how you handle emotions? Write in the space below any responses you have to these questions.

Letting Go of Blame

Blame is a virus, destroying our Vision, harming our well-being, keeps us in the past, and is bred in a false reality that we don't have power or are not in control. We all at times have blamed, and it can curb our life when we hold onto deep-seated thoughts about someone whom we believe is responsible for our pain.

My teacher would tell the story of two monks when he would talk about blame;

That there was an elder monk and a younger monk walking down and going towards a temple and on the way they had a very shallow river, very shallow river to cross. But on the bank of the river that they're going to walk through there was a young woman, beautifully dressed and she did not know how to cross the river because her whole dress would get wet. So, the older monk picked her up in his arms and then crossed the river with her. He dropped her off when he crossed the river, on the bank. And they continued walking, the elder monk and the younger monk. The younger monk did not say a single word. He had an angry look.

The elder monk asked, "What happened?"

He said, "You shouldn't have picked up that beautiful woman like that in your arms and crossed the river."

The elder monk looked at him very affectionately and said, "I dropped her on the bank of the river and you're still carrying her."

He would go on to say;

If you ever blame anybody for anything, you're only exposing your own weakness, own incompetency, and your own shortcomings. Doesn't matter if it's your own parent, your friend, or your colleague. Don't blame.

That includes ourselves. Imagine you never blamed another, including yourself.

Write down someone or something you blame.

_____
_____

Drawing to mind the first thought about your subject of blame, what is the story of that thought?

_____
_____
_____

The event or individual that you blame exists independent of the meaning you place on it or them. It exists simply as an event. It is our thought which is a story about protecting ourselves, a defense from feeling unsafe, that gives meaning to the individual or event we blame. Ask what are you protecting yourself from?

_____
_____
_____

Is there another story that you are not considering, about yourself, the other, or anyone else involved with your event?

_____
_____
_____

Be compassionate as you answer as we are not trying to deflect blame on to yourself, but instead we want to witness the event objectively.

What was learned from this event?

_____
_____

True healing from blame comes when we see our response as a choice. Someone might have duped you, hurt you, or caused you pain, but the ability to do those things existed in you.

You are the cause of your own experience, we all are, and all the experiences you have given yourself were perfect for the creation of who you choose to Be.

This is an incredible sense of responsibility for us as Creators. I know many people, when they hear that they have created the events in their life, first think about all the pains that they have endured and become angry because there is no way they created their pain. That responsibility is too great for some, therefore we hold onto our pains by blaming others for them.

Source, our Consciousness, exists on a level above our pains and hardships, and uses them as a tool of creation to build Self, which we will get into a little later.

If you still can't let go of blame, then choose to forgive.

Forgiveness

If we are blaming then we are not forgiving. When we don't forgive we hold on to the hurt or pain, which affects our well-being. Yet when we forgive, we let go, and when we let go, we heal.

Forgiving doesn't mean we let others harm us, as we are not martyrs. We defend ourselves from hurt but we forgive any that has been caused - we are forgiving the person, not condoning behaviour.

We don't forgive for the other but for ourselves. As Alan Brandt the historian once said, *Resentment is like taking poison and hoping it'll kill someone else.* Forgiving can be very hard to do, but if we are not willing to, it does not affect the other person.

Do you have someone you need to forgive?

First ask yourself if you can forgive, honestly, and do you want to? Write your response below.

When we can't forgive it is because it gives us power. Ask yourself why it's important for you to hold that power?

What are you protecting yourself from?

_____

_____

Try this powerful exercise that helps us forgive those who we frame as having caused our pain:

In a meditation pose, close your eyes and breathe into your heart. Think about that pain the other person caused you. Feel the hurt, the anger, maybe even the frustration. Now imagine the other person and notice that they don't experience these feelings you do. Your holding onto the feelings doesn't affect the other person, only you. Only you carry the feelings. Reflect on this. Now see the situation that caused your stress from the others perspective. What's their character or cultural background that affected the outcome of the hurtful action? What was their mood? Think how the actions of the other were based on their circumstances and upbringing. Seeing the other, feeling the pain that was only experienced by you, and the other perspective of the hurter, now say, 'I forgive you. I forgive you. I forgive you.' Lastly, have kindness and compassion for yourself. As you take time coming out of this meditation breath in kindness and compassion for yourself.

Forgiveness is a powerful place to love from.

When you look deeply into your anger, you will see that the person you call your enemy is also suffering. As soon as you see that, the capacity of accepting and having compassion for them is there.
    - Thich Nhat Hanh

Approaching Fear

If we are blaming and unable to forgive, it could be because of something we fear.
Maybe in the above exercises a lingering fear came to your awareness, or maybe you can think of some fears you have now. Is there a fear that you are holding on to in the background of your life that drives your thoughts. Looking at what causes our fear is sometimes enough to move through it.

First, we are going to look at how our fears manifested in the past. Write below an event that has already happened that you feared before it occurred.

_____

_____

After what you feared had passed what happened? How did your life change?
___
___
___

Reflecting on this event that you feared, and looking at how it turned out, what did you learn?
___
___
___

Below is an exercise to see what would happen if your fears were realized. Take something you're scared about, a future event that makes you afraid, and try this exercise.

The fear: ___

If it occurs, what do you believe will happen as a result?
___
___

What would happen after that?
___

And what would happen after that?
___

And what would happen after that?
___

And what would happen after that?
___

What then are you ultimately afraid of?
___
___
___

Adapted from the *Conversations with God Guidebook (1997)*

If we just look at our fears directly, at their outcomes, sometimes it's enough to eliminate much of the fear itself.

Experience the Ocean of the Mind

If after all these exercises, in attempting to gain awareness of your limiting beliefs, hurts, and pains, and you're still finding yourself unable to change challenging thoughts or behavior, try the Ocean of the Mind exercise.

This is an exercise to experience your own Ocean of the Mind, very similar to the one I experienced in my fourth contact event, in which I was connected to a device that projected a hologram of a cross section of an ocean symbolizing the mind's depth.

This exercise works well when you have trouble understanding the origin or motivation behind behaviors or thought patterns, and want to bring awareness to them either out of self-exploration, or because they limit you or cause you pain.

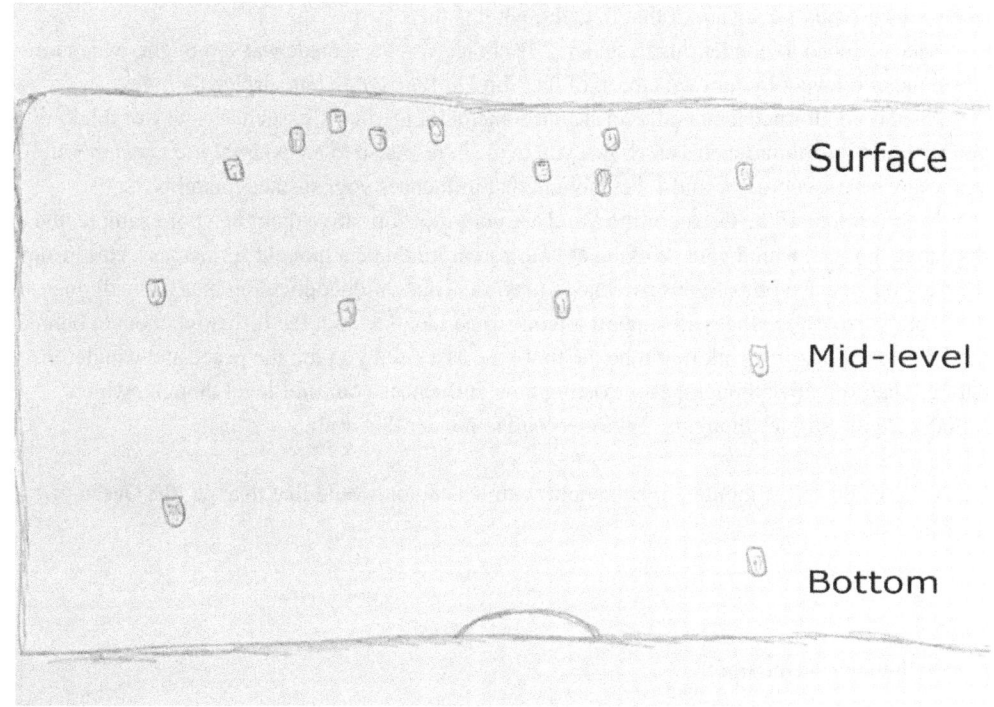

The Ocean of the Mind

Take a second to observe the above diagram. Imagine how this can represent your own mind. Notice the floating rectangles – look at one and think of a thought you had recently. Imagine that thought is the floating rectangle. Now, take a second to imagine that those objects floating at the surface are the thoughts you've had over the last hour. Briefly reflect over the last hour what you did, and loosely imagine all those thoughts that occurred are floating there on the surface. These thoughts on the surface are those that you are aware of at the present moment. Those thoughts that your conscious mind will see and reflect on. See them there if you can.

Now observe the mid-level. These thoughts are those that are historical, containing life choices that you have made. For example, wherever you are, or whatever you are doing right now, is governed by an initial choice – a first thought about putting yourself where you are. Let's say it's your work; the mid-level thought is not that which brough you to work today, such as "I gotta go to work to pay the bills." It's the initial thought about that job, the choice you made to take that job, the reason you did, and the thoughts you had about wanting that job; these are the thoughts at the mid-level. Or lets say you are currently reading this in a park; the thought at the mid-level would be about the initial thought you have about relaxing in parks, the first thought about the enjoyment you can have from relaxing in parks, which probably occurred many years ago. Well, that thought is currently sitting in your subconscious, "colouring" the surface thoughts, those thoughts which you are aware of at the top of the Ocean of the Mind. You most likely are currently not aware of that thought, but it is there.

Take a second to ponder this truth; any life choice you have made was a thought, which now sits at the mid-level of your own Ocean of the Mind, influencing your surface thoughts.

Also, if you formed a mental tendency at some point in your life, such as a way of thinking, you will find its origins, such as a choice you made in response to an external life event, possibly years ago, here as a present mid-level thought that influences your surface thoughts.

At the bottom of the Ocean of the Mind are your root/formative thoughts. For example, the formative thought behind your working at your career might be a thought formed as a child from the day you watched one of your parents go to work. That childhood feeling that you will one day proudly have a job that will support a family, just like them. Or the formative thought behind your desire to relax in a park might be the first time as a child you felt the peace and wonder of nature. That formative thought, also existing now, influences your mid-level thought, which influences your surface thoughts. Take a second to ponder this truth.

Below, write down the thought or behaviour with which you would like to apply the Ocean of the Mind to.

Now follow this meditation:

Close your eyes and take a deep breath. When you're ready, picture in your mind's eye the image of the Ocean of the Mind, the cross section of an ocean, so that you are looking at it in three layers. Just sit with this image. See the surface waves and how exposed the surface of the ocean is. Then bring your attention to the middle of the ocean and feel the large body of water. It can be so large it can have its own current. It can be moving and shifting all on its own, separate from the surface. Now see the ocean depth, maybe it's dark for you, and deep. It's the depth of you.

Now see the entire Ocean of the Mind. Now bring your attention to the thought pattern or behaviour that you would like to change. Remind yourself of a moment that occurred recently in which you were living those thoughts or behaviours.

Now see the thoughts, or the thoughts that control that behaviour, floating on the surface. Just see the thoughts anyway you can, floating there. Maybe they are images. Just see those thoughts anyway you can.

Slowly bring your gaze to the mid-level thoughts. Feel that these thoughts and their roots go deeper into your subconscious. Take note of whatever thoughts come to mind.

Now slowly bring your attention to the bottom of the ocean, to the lower-level thoughts.

What images or thoughts do you see there? What images or thoughts seem connected to the thoughts at the top? What comes to mind? What moment in time created that thought? What moment of time or event is this thought showing you?

Bring awareness to this image, time, or feelings, and simply make a note of it.

Now slowly, taking your time, come out of this meditation.

Write here what image, moment in time, or thoughts was at the mid-level of the ocean for you?

_____
_____
_____
_____
_____

Write here what image, moment in time, or thoughts was at the bottom of the ocean for you?

_____
_____
_____
_____
_____

Now remove any judgment or expectation of this old image or thought and just observe it - have total acceptance. Come to a place of compassion, and love for yourself.

After you have grounded yourself in compassion, come back to this deep-seated thought. Can you create a new perspective of that old thought? Can you see it objectively, remove blame, forgive, see the story it creates for you, or the story from someone else's perspective? Can you see how this has shaped you with learning that you otherwise wouldn't have gained? If you need to, take this awareness of your old thought and reread the above sections, starting at *Handling our Emotions,* as a way of healing the newly revealed feelings and images.

Taking Time to Reflect

Now that we have gone deep, pulling out thought patterns and layers of conditioning, you have emptied the cup, now it's time to fill it. But before we do, give yourself time to reflect.

Taking time to reflect, at least 10-15 minutes, several times a week, gives the brain an opportunity to process information and emotions, allowing you to clarify your intentions, and verbalize your thoughts and feelings. It should be in a supportive environment, away from work or distracting technology, and when your mind is open.

There are various ways in which we can take time to reflect, such as by talking to yourself, through reflective writing, or by walking.

When we walk as a form of reflection, research shows that we decrease rational and linear thinking and increase divergent and imaginative mind-wandering. Many have long known walking to be an aid to thinking such as Philosopher Friedrich Nietzsche who in 1889 wrote *All truly great thoughts are conceived by walking.*

Rejuvenating Emotional Energy

Now that we have explored several challenging emotional topics, it is important to focus on being positive. We can be positive when we have positive emotional energy.

Feeling filled with emotional energy makes us happy, and when we carry this energy in our hearts, we feel we are in a flow. Positive energy will feel like you carry a background sense of contentment, happiness, peace, or even joy.

Try for a day to observe your energy levels, you'll be surprised at what you will find - make a note in the morning, afternoon, and evening. What do you find when you give yourself a moment to reflect on your energy level? For example, when was your energy highest and what made it so? When was your energy the lowest and do you know what was its cause?

When we know what drains our emotional energy, we are then able to make lifestyle choices that focus on the things with which boost our emotional energy.

Emotions will always be a part of our human world, so we need to embrace them and make them work for us. Below are some tips for having healthy emotional energy.

The Basics: Though most probably don't need to hear the health benefits of a healthy diet, physical exercise, sufficient rest, sleep, spending time in nature, and having a clean home environment, but it is important to mention that these are connected to our emotional well-being. Sometimes a low emotional state can be changed by focusing on one of the above.

Think positively: Negative thinking is an emotional energy drainer, so be vigilant at noticing when your mind drifts into negative thinking. When I catch myself thinking negatively, I'll replay the thought or scenario in my mind, redoing the version where I think positively, erasing the effects of the negative thinking on my emotional energy.

Self-Encouragement: Pay attention to your internal dialogue, and the words you say to yourself in your mind. Try changing your internal dialogue with yourself so that it is encouraging and complimentary.

Drop the technology: Smartphones, computers, and TV, can be a drain on emotional energy. Try for a night to stay off your smartphone, computer, and TV. Let yourself be bored and see what happens. You'll find that the lack of technology for the night will energize you.

Watch the Sky: In ecopsychology research, watching the sky has been associated with reduced stress, and induced natural contemplation, which has been shown to help the brain organize emotions. Whether it's the blue sky, clouds, or star gazing, spend time to watch the sky.

Smile: Smiles are known for psychologically increasing mood, even if you're not feeling well. The psychologist James D. Laird showed that when the facial muscles were used to create a smile, that part of the brain that registered happiness lit up. Even a fake smile can strengthen the brain's neural outlook on life. Therefore, the simplest way to make one happy is to smile.

Laughter: Laughter therapy is scientifically supported and known to reduce stress and anxiety. It can involve acting silly, being playful, or watching a funny movie, but laughter can also be naturally induced, by just beginning to, well...laugh for no reason.

Singing: Singing has been linked to increased well-being. Sing when you're alone, in the car, or with others. Also, playing, listening, and dancing to music are all associated with greater well-being.

Do something different: Break up your habits a little; drive to work choosing a different way, have something new for dinner, or give yourself small adventures.

Connect with the Present: When we are not thinking about the past or future, we are typically not expending our energy. Present moment focus allows us to connect to ourselves and re-energize.

Breath: From our section on meditation, breathe into your belly through your nose, let it pause, and exhale out through your nose, let it pause. Breath is powerful for boosting emotional energy.

Meditation: Another great method for revitalizing our emotional energy is with a focused meditation. When I was working in the bank and had to punch in overtime hours, just to get the work done, I would go into the lunchroom and do a quick one-minute power meditation, focusing on my breath and seeing a dot on my third eye. Very quickly, it would clear the exhaustion from my brain and energize me for another hour of work.

Gratefulness

"We can only be said to be alive in those moments when our hearts are conscious of our treasures."
   - Thornton Wilder

   Gratefulness is a powerful attitude that can change our focus from what we don't have to what we do have. Even if things in your life are hard, frustrating, or you are low in energy, think about the things with which you are grateful for, and it will ground and energize you.
   In positive psychology gratefulness is seen as a very powerful attitude for creating a positive feedback loop - when we receive or express gratitude, we create a desire for more of what we are grateful for. So, try these exercises below to increase your gratitude.

Write down three things you are grateful for:

   1._____

   2._____

   3._____

Write down three things you are grateful for today:

1. _____

2. _____

3. _____

Write down three things you are grateful for that will occur in the near future. Could be anything, such as coming home to your family after work, or an event you find special.

1. _____

2. _____

3. _____

Now, when the thing you are grateful for happens, remind yourself in the moment of your gratefulness.

Try feeling grateful for something you don't normally feel grateful for. Maybe it is regarding your work, a relationship, or an experience. Think of as many things you can be grateful for about that thing.

_____
_____
_____
_____

How did it feel to do this last exercise?

_____
_____
_____

The attitude of your gratitude determines your altitude.
  - Maharaj

Begin cultivating an attitude of gratefulness, of which there are many different ways to do so; you could repeat the above exercises several times a week, you could focus on gratitude during your meditation, or at the end of the day you could remind yourself what you were grateful for. Do what suits you best. By cultivating gratitude, you will begin hardwiring your brain for a kinder and more positive outlook on life.

A Self-Loving Exercise

In all relationships it starts with ourselves. We cannot love anybody else without first loving ourselves. We are the tool with which we learn how to love others. Our ability to forgive, to be compassionate, to accept, to let others grow, starts with ourselves. To give us the freedom of unconditional love allows us to unconditionally love others.

We want to bring ourselves to a mindful place of recognizing our negative self-thoughts are stories, and only stories, and most likely made of false information. Be compassionate with yourself. In reality, would you ever have that same internal language you have with yourself with a friend. Let go of the perfectionist to know there is perfection in being who you are and that any human would do the so-called "mess up," "mistake," or "error." This helps us to be objective when as roommates with ourselves we typically are subjective, judging our reactions and expecting greater results than we would have with another.

To develop a healthy mental attitude towards yourself, think about a difficult situation that you may have been hard on yourself with, and describe it below. Make a note of your thoughts and bodily sensations as you describe it.

_____
_____
_____
_____

Now being objective, can you see how anyone else, in your exact scenario, would have reacted the same. Try to adopt an attitude that is kind, compassionate, and caring to yourself. If you can't do this, then let your thoughts pass on as clouds. Or try talking with yourself, being the compassionate person you might be with another.

Repeat your name, forgiving yourself, even if you don't have anything to forgive yourself for, just repeat this phrase. For example; *Sophia, I forgive you*, repeated.
Make a note of how it feels to say this to yourself.

_____
_____
_____

For these next exercises, put yourself in front of a mirror. Now, looking at yourself in the mirror, what are your three best physical attributes? Write those down.

1) _____

2) _____

3) _____

Again looking at yourself, what are your three best mental attributes? Write those down.

1) _____

2) _____

3) _____

Again looking at yourself, this time make sure you look into your eyes, what are the three best attributes of your spirit? Write those down.

1) _____

2) _____

3) _____

Again, looking into a mirror, say;

"I love this person. I know all of your fallacies and yet I still love you. What you think are imperfections are not really imperfections at all, but a process of the soul. I know you try your best. I love you. I love you. I forgive you and I love you."

Now repeat this line three times; "I am sent by the Unified Field Force. I am sent by my Higher Self. I am."

What can you do right now that makes you feel like you cherish yourself?

___

What does it look like in your mind's eye to truly fall in love with your Self? What would you do differently? Sit quietly and think about this. Write down your answer when you're ready.

___

If any of this was challenging, no problem, this is common, as it can be hard to feel affection for ourselves. Be patient with yourself.

We all simply want to love and be loved, and that includes you. Any perceived imperfections about yourself, with which you can create judgment about, can be boiled down to this desire - the desire to love and be loved. There is freedom in this discovery.

The Second Proclamation

Experiencing our Consciousness starts with the recognition of our Source. We are One and the same with Source, yet our mind and our environment makes this a challenge to absorb. The purpose of the second proclamation is to experience that everything around you is Consciousness, is Source, and that you are connected to it.

I introduce an ancient Sanskrit dictum as the second proclamation; **Tat Tavm Asi** (Source: Samaveda, Chandogya Upanishad 6.8.7).

Phonetically it is;

Tat Tavum Asee

Tat means That, *Tavm* means Thou, and *Asi* means Are or Art. Therefore, the meaning of this proclamation is That Thou Art - Source/Consciousness is all things. It means we are connected to all things. Consciousness is everything including all that you hear, see, touch, taste, and smell.

We may think of Source as a blind mechanical energy, but this perspective is too limiting. Consciousness, Source, is not just the all-pervading energy, but is also alive, meaning it is intelligent, and it is the root of our awareness.

Repeat this Proclamation in your meditation by breathing in through your nose and on your exhale, say Tat Tavum Asee by elongating the vowels; not too fast and not too slow.

This proclamation imbues in you the feeling of Oneness. *The Creator and the Created are One and the same,* as my teacher says.

Within each we are One and the same yet we have become conditioned to believing we are separate. Unity will feel like; when the leaves of the trees rustle it is happening in your heart, when the birds chirp it is an expression of the heart inside you, that the objects you see and hear are connected to you, that you can feel yourself in the land and mountains. The more Tat Tavum Asi is meditated upon, over time, this experience will grow inside you.

However, Unity can happen for you, it is your birthright - our love and joy lives here. Unity expands our experience of love to the love of all things, and to the love of life.

If this is new to you, you may find it easier to experience connection in nature. While in nature, bring your awareness to something, such as a tree, or flower, or the landscape, or the Earth. See if you can connect to it in your heart. Try loving the thing you're looking at. Close your eyes if you need to. Be aware of what your feeling, and don't force anything. Smell the air, connect to the environment and repeat Tat Tavm Asi - declare your connection.

Lastly, seeking Unity, knowing we are connected, puts the focus of your mind on your heart while you engage with the external world. It's the change of focus from "out there," to "in here" while I deal with "out there."

Seeing Source in All Things

When I connect to the present, I feel it in my heart. I see everything as an expression of Source and look for the vibrancy in the world around me. Can I see something I hadn't noticed before? I become aware of how inanimate objects can feel as if they have a life of their own, or I take notice of the empty space in a room. As I become aware of Source, my heart feels love, and in a fluid experience I can feel me in whatever I focus on. The deep sensations in me of Unity are not happening in a thought of any future event or past activity, they happen here and Now.

Right now, what do you hear? That is Consciousness. What do you see? That is Consciousness. What are you touching? That is Consciousness. What do you taste? That is Consciousness. What do you smell? That is Consciousness.

Name three random objects in your vicinity.

_____

_____

_____

Take a moment to ponder that these objects are Source.

Think of three objects you have fond memories of, that you might be attached to.

_____
_____
_____

Take a moment to ponder that these objects are Source.

Make a list of the top five things that you would say supports you to live on the physical level. For example; your home, car, food, etc.

_____
_____
_____
_____
_____

Now think about each one, and as you do, repeat Tat Tavm Asi. How does it feel to do this exercise?

_____
_____
_____

    Wonder, awe, amazement, and mystery live in your world now, no matter how mundane you believe it to be. The mystery of Source surrounds us while being everything in our lives. See the world around you, the ever-present moment of Now, with the wonder of a child.

    As you move your body, repeat Tat Tavm Asi, feeling Source as the energy that moves it. Moving slowly, deliberately, and with an open mind, become aware of the full experience of your body, this marvelous machine, bones, and muscle, holding you up right. Feel your breath move through your body. Notice the sensations in your feet, how your weight changes the feelings. Keep your attention on what you're doing, repeating Tat Tavm Asi.

    Try experiencing Source by watching a clear starry night sky. The great cosmos is alive with Source - the magnificent expanse. Look at a single star and see with wonder and amazement that you're looking out into our massive galaxy. Maybe you can feel the planet beneath your feet as it's floating in space, the way the sunlight hits the moon, emphasizing the tilt of the Earth, as you face into the starry Universe.

> *Everything that you hear is an extension of you*
> *Everything that you see is an extension of you.*

4 Steps to Connect with Source

1) Become aware of your surroundings and find something you have never noticed before. What do you hear? What do you smell? What do you feel on your skin?
2) Connect to your feeling. An energy permeates the environment you are in, see if you can feel it in your heart. Close your eyes if you need to.
3) Become aware that Source is all that is surrounding you. Repeat Tat Tavm Asi. Focus on something in your environment and see it as Source.
4) Whatever may be supporting you in your environment, see it as Source. For example, the chair that is holding you up, the food you're eating that is nourishing you, the ground that you walk on. Whatever it is, see it as Source supporting you, helping you.

Intuition & The Dimensionality of Consciousness

In this section we seek to attain an experience of our expanded Consciousness - our higher awareness. We are reclaiming our heritage, our intuition, the part of us that is beyond space and time.

You will be shown several different techniques to experience your expanded Consciousness, so you can figure out what works for you. This discovery is personal, with different individuals requiring different frames of reference, modalities, or explanations to open this part of the Self.

There is no easy way to open up our energy, intuition, and dimensional sides, but try using these techniques to shift your awareness. If you want to, you will experience it. If you truly have the desire from your heart, it will happen.

The Vibratory Nature of Energy

God moves in cycles. Consciousness moves in cycles, and you humans in your collective Consciousness move in cycles.
  -*The Mystic Book*

All of nature is cyclical; birth and death, night and day, summer and winter. And everything in nature contains a centrifugal and centripetal; expanding and contracting, active and receptive, male and female, positive and negative. This is the great duality.

The energy that permeates our world moves in a cycle, much like our breath, expanding out in a positive phase, and coming back in a negative phase or polarity. But there is also the neutral phase or polarity, much like the pause in between our breaths.

In Vedic Philosophy, these three principles are called Sattva Guna (neutral), Rajas Guna (positive), and Tamas Guna (negative). The word Guna is Sanskrit for twirl or wind, thus describing the vortices of vibrating energy fields.

The Universe's emanations, vibratory by nature, can be experienced as the impressions and feelings from the objects, environment, or people around us. We can feel this vibration from others, even when we are not aware of it. When we say we "don't like their vibe" we are in fact reading a person's energy field and deciding if it resonates with our own.

The energy that permeates everything can be thought of as vibrations, vortexes, an energy field, Consciousness (just like you), or as the aware unified field force of the Universe, whatever suits you.

Water makes for an astute analogy for energy. Here is a meditation where we visualize ourselves as water, as a way of awakening our energetic vibratory nature.

Water Meditation

Close your eyes. Take a deep breath through your nose, into your belly, and exhale. Sit quietly and feel the rhythm of your breath. Now imagine a mountain brook, a small stream in the mountains. See the water forming pools, running over rocks, trickling, making its sounds, flowing down the mountain.

Now imagine this little brook is you. You are the water, flowing over the rocks, forming in pools, and trickling down the mountain. Feel this anyway you can. Try to experience this any way that works for you. Maybe it's that you just see your face over the water. Maybe you can feel in your imagination that you can be fluid just like water. Anyway, this works for you. Just try to connect that the water you're seeing coming down the mountain is you. You are flowing over rocks, morphing around them, over sticks, and under logs, forming into pools, then continuing to trickle downwards.

Ahead you see the brook connects to a large flowing river. As you merge from the brook to this river, you become it, flowing, moving, shaping around boulders, meandering through landscapes of wilderness. Feel the waves are your vibrations.

Then you see a large waterfall approaching. You're the body of water, flowing over the edge, as you briefly become the waterfall. You come crashing down unaffected by the tumult, into a large pool of water, and continue to flow.

Now ahead is even a larger river with which you merge. Your body is now wide and fluid, with waves forming on the top of you, flowing over top of boulders underneath that can't even be seen from the surface. Feel the waves are your vibrations.

Ahead of you is the ocean. As you leave the river and come to the ocean, you merge. Feel the immense size of your body - how fluid the slow, wavy movement. Feel the surface waves are your vibrations.

Take a moment to absorb this experience.

Now over top of you is a beautiful blue sky with the dazzling Sun in the center. See it there over top of you, with the light sparkling on the surface of your body. See the light sparkling its golden white light as it reflects off your body.

Take a moment to absorb this experience.

Now, still with your eyes closed, slowly come out of this meditation by bringing your awareness back to your body and placing your hands on the ground as a means for grounding. Take a few deep breaths and come on out and open your eyes.

Write here what you experienced.

_____
_____
_____
_____
_____
_____

How Consciousness Is Interpreted by the Brain

How we label what we experience determines how we experience it. Our internal dialogue, thoughts, and images associated with any experience of Consciousness colours what we think it means to have that experience.

The Oxford Dictionary (2023) definition of psychic is;

Relating to or denoting faculties or phenomena that are apparently inexplicable by natural laws, especially involving telepathy or clairvoyance.

The Wikipedia (2023) definition of Extra Sensory Perception (ESP) is;

Extrasensory perception or ESP, also called sixth sense, is a claimed paranormal ability pertaining to reception of information not gained through the recognized physical senses but sensed with the mind.

The Oxford Dictionary (2023) definition of intuition is;

The ability to understand something immediately, without the need for conscious reasoning.

Psychic abilities, ESP, and intuition are moments when the brain gains awareness and/or receives information from an expanded experience of Consciousness, which resides in no space and no time. When we feel someone is about to text us, that is no space, as we can feel them, in their locality, regardless of distance, thinking about us. When we wake up with a funny feeling about the day, and then midday something goes wrong at our job, that's no time, as we were aware of something before it was even set in motion.

So, for this reason I don't use the word psychic, may use intuition, but will largely use dimensionality, expanded/extended Consciousness, or just Consciousness. How we label it subconsciously colours our experience of it, and since the experience of Consciousness is multifaceted and specific to each individual, we will simply refer to it as our dimensional capabilities.

It's really just personal preference. I like to lean towards a simple understanding that all the different experiences of Consciousness are simply just Consciousness. It allows us to accept this larger version of ourselves.

Our brain processes the energy of Consciousness and its frequencies through our five senses, and we perceive its energetic signatures through those senses which are most open to us. We can experience energy and our extended Consciousness as colour, texture, taste, or even smell. As we grew up as children and teenagers, we relied on the different senses which formed our cognitive style. A cognitive style is your mode of perceiving, thinking, remembering, learning, and problem solving. Each of us has a cognitive style with which our brain is wired.

It's not a hard and fast rule, but you will likely find your experience of energy and extended Consciousness to be extensions of your personal cognitive styles. I refer to them here as a general guide to help you. If you're new to these ideas of extended Consciousness, then hopefully it will provide some comfort that its experience can be unique for everyone.

Audio Cognitive Style

Someone with an audio cognitive style will be sensitive to sounds and music, may prefer spoken instructions as opposed to written, and will remember things by how they sounded.

Their expanded Consciousness could be experienced through clairaudience, which is gaining extra-sensory information through audio. Or it can be experienced as a real voice, or impressions translated into words in one's own mind in the speech center of the brain. Consciousness might speak to them through a ringing or changes in the ear. Or they could sometimes hear a specific song that they know, with lyrics that act as a message, and it could come into their head just at the right time that they are seeking guidance.

Spatial Cognitive Style

Someone with a spatial cognitive stye will be good at directions, will know how to geographically orient themselves, and be able to imagine the dimensions of other physical environments.

They may experience their expanded Consciousness through feeling the energy of an environment, such as in rooms, buildings, or Earth energies, and will have a natural intuition for concepts like good feng shui. Consciousness may speak to them while looking at a map, directing them to go to a significant location.

Empathic Cognitive Style

Someone with an empathic cognitive stye will feel the emotions of other people. When extended in Consciousness empaths can feel the events, or life issues of others, from a distance or before they happen.

Somatic Cognitive Style

Someone with a somatic cognitive style will be sensitive to the feelings in their body. Our body is its own organism, with its own intuitive intelligence knowing what is real, therefore Consciousness may express itself in clear visceral guidance. They may be able to quickly heal themselves, or understand what emotions or thoughts caused their ailment. Combined with empathy, they might feel a physical ailment of another in their own body.

Kinesthetic-Tactile Cognitive Style

Someone with a kinesthetic-tactile cognitive style will like to touch things. While shopping they may need to pick things up and feel them before they buy it. With expanded Consciousness it can manifest as psychometry, which is seeing the history of an object once it has been touched.

Visual Cognitive Style

Someone with a visual cognitive style will typically love art, or photography, and could also be a visual learner. With expanded Consciousness information can come from visual images or symbols, much like a dream, meaning it could take time to figure out what the symbology means. You can refer back to the dream section for that.

Near Death Experiences

There are many other things that open up different types of experiences of Consciousness, such as having a near death experience. People who have a near death experience, or who have seen the afterlife, often end up with the ability to hear other spirits. It may also manifest in knowing when someone is going to die.

In summary, this guide is meant to show that Consciousness and its dimensionality can manifest in many different ways for people. If you identify with any of the above cognitive styles, consider its associated expanded Consciousness description as a way it could manifest for you as we explore the exercises. If any of them don't work for you, try modifying it towards one of your cognitive styles and see if that helps.

The Energy of Our Body

A good place to start with our experience of energy is with the body's energy field. The body itself is a field of Consciousness, with an energy of awareness permeating throughout it. The human energy field of the Self extends outside our body, about a foot off of the skin (though thinner fabrics of energy extend out in the environment). Thoughts and emotions can lodge there and if we don't know how to release them they can manifest as physical ailments. These thoughts and feelings lodged in the extended energy field, commonly called an aura, can be sensed, and cleared by those who know how to do so. This is the practice of Reiki.

Take a second to feel your energy around your body.

Try this body scan meditation to help bring awareness to your body's energy.

Body Scan Meditation

Start by lying down on your back, with your legs slightly apart, arms at your side, and palms facing downwards. It's important though to be comfortable. Notice your breath, bringing yourself into the moment and just accept what you're feeling and what comes up for you.

Now close your eyes and bring your attention to your toes. Feel whatever sensations you can feel. If you can't feel any sensation, just be aware of the lack of sensation. Feel your breath and imagine you are breathing into your toes. Gradually move your attention to your feet. Keep your attention here and feel whatever sensations you can feel. Again, feel your breath and imagine you are breathing into your feet. Do this for every body part as we slowly move up. Bring your attention to your lower legs. Feel your calves. Keep your attention here and feel whatever sensations you can feel. Imagine you are breathing into your calves. Feel your shins. Keep your attention here and feel whatever sensations you can feel. Imagine you are breathing into your shins. Sit with this feeling. Breathe into them. Then bring your awareness to your kneecaps. Feel your kneecaps. Keep your attention here and feel whatever sensations you can feel. Imagine you are breathing into your kneecaps. Then slowly bring your awareness to your thighs. Keep your attention here and feel whatever sensations you can feel. Imagine you are breathing into your thighs. Feel the muscles that make up your thighs. Maybe you can feel the clothes you're wearing on your skin. Then slowly bring your attention to your pelvis. Keep your attention here and feel whatever sensations you can feel. Imagine you are breathing into your pelvis. Breathe into your pelvis. Feel your buttocks touching the ground or whatever you're lying on. Keep your attention here and feel whatever sensations you can feel. Imagine you are breathing into your buttocks. Then bring your awareness to your belly. Keep your attention here and feel whatever sensations you can feel. Imagine you are breathing into your belly. Try and see if you can bring your attention to your intestines. Feel inside your belly and feel your intestines. Just observe the feelings and sensations. Now bring your attention to your chest. First, feel the sensation of your rib cage. Keep your attention here and feel whatever sensations you can feel. Imagine you are breathing into your rib cage. Just sit with the awareness. Then slowly bring your awareness to your heart. Keep your attention here and feel whatever sensations you can feel. Imagine you are breathing into your heart. Feeling it pumping. Just observe. Now, become aware of your lungs. Keep your attention here and feel whatever sensations you can feel. Breathe into your lungs. Feel them move up and down as they fill up with air and then release carbon dioxide. Now bring your awareness to your spine. Keep your attention here and feel whatever sensations you can feel. Imagine you are breathing into your spine. Feel its length, from the base of your spine, up behind your belly, your lower back, up behind your heart, your middle back, to the back of your neck.

Now bring your attention to your shoulders. Keep your attention here and feel whatever sensations you can feel. Imagine you are breathing into your shoulders. Feel any clothes they may be touching. Now bring your attention to your arms. Keep your attention here and feel whatever sensations you can feel. Imagine you are breathing into your arms. Feel your biceps. Keep your attention here and feel whatever sensations you can feel. Imagine you are breathing into your biceps. Slowly bring your attention to your forearms. Keep your attention here and feel whatever sensations you can feel. Imagine you are breathing into your forearms. Feel the skin. Then feel your hands. Keep your attention here and feel whatever sensations you can feel. Imagine you are breathing into your hands. Become aware of the muscles, and the sensations of your hands. Just sit with these sensations.

Now bring your awareness to your neck. Keep your attention here and feel whatever sensations you can feel. Imagine you are breathing into your neck. Feel your throat. Feel the back of your neck attached to your head. Now feel your head. Keep your attention here and feel whatever sensations you can feel. Imagine you are breathing into your head. Feel your tongue in your mouth. Keep your attention here and feel whatever sensations you can feel. Imagine you are breathing into your tongue. Feel your teeth. Keep your attention here and feel whatever sensations you can feel. Imagine you are breathing into your teeth. Feel your nose. Keep your attention here and feel whatever sensations you can feel. Imagine you are breathing into your nose. Become aware of the sensation of your eyes. Keep your attention here and feel whatever sensations you can feel. Imagine you are breathing into your eyes. Now bring your awareness to your brain inside your head. Keep your attention here and feel whatever sensations you can feel. Imagine you are breathing into your brain. Feel the inside of your head.

Now just sit with the feelings in your body. Just rest in the feeling of your body.

When you're done, open your eyes and get up slowly, being aware of the sensations in your body as you do.

Write here what this experience was like for you.

_____
_____
_____
_____

Grounding our Electromagnetic Fields

A natural electromagnetic field permeates through nature which can be felt, and when we connect to it we can feel our own energy field.

Try this 15-minute tree meditation.

Find a place in nature filled with trees, preferably land that hasn't been disturbed by man, such as an old growth forest, but if this is not available to you, no problem as this exercise will work with any land.

Choose an older tree, as opposed to a sapling, and make sure it hasn't suffered trauma such as having been engraved, cut, or burnt.

For 5 minutes (use a timer if required) rest your forehead, closer to the fontanel (the soft spot on the top of your head) on the tree, as if you are prostrating before it, with hands flat against it, while repeating Tat Tavm Asi, as you would during meditation (though any mantra or positive meditation will work).

Then for 5 minutes, place your heart against the tree, as if you are hugging it, while repeating your meditation.

Then for 5 minutes, place your spine against the tree, with the back of your head, and hands flat against it, while repeating your meditation.

If there is any discomfort take a break, breathe into your belly and repeat a proclamation to ground yourself.

If all of the above was followed you will feel a shift in the electromagnetic field in your body - this is the feeling of energy.

This is known as "grounding" and is the process of connecting your electromagnetic field to the Earths. Research has shown it to be beneficial to our bodies and I can attest that it has cured my headaches, colds, and helped me gain clear thinking over complex emotional issues.

Sensing and Feeling With Our Being

Yet who you really are is a quantum dimensional Consciousness experienced as pure Being and pure feeling.
    -The Mystic Book

Having established that Consciousness is energy, and that our experience of this is our pure Being and pure feeling, try to imagine that this portion of you can sense, feel, and "see" with its own eyes; it can do this in any environment, with the rooms that you walk into, and with the people that you meet.

What is required is a sensitivity that is akin to ourselves as a child. When we were younger, we were often told that we were too sensitive. Maybe you were told to quit crying, or stop daydreaming, or settle down if you came into a room with childlike exuberance. These messages are our childhood programming.

In the last chapter we talked about coming to the world around us with the eyes of a child. Feel free to take a moment to review that section *The Amazement and Wonder of the Now*. For our work here we want to give ourselves permission to be as sensitive as we can be. Our experience of energy is felt in the subtle experiences of our heart, and we were open to these subtle experiences when our hearts were open with the sensitivity of a child. Breathe into your heart and allow yourself to be sensitive again.

Take a moment to ponder that you can sense, and listen with your Being, with your feeling. Can you pick up the feel that is in the air? Can you sense the vibrations coming off of your friend? Right now, close your eyes and feel your environment. Did you notice, "pick up," or sense anything?

When our intuition speaks it will be with our first feeling before it is interpreted by the mind - this is pure feeling. The question then becomes how do we get the mind out of the way?

You might experience a message from pure Consciousness in a subconscious flow state, also called a hypnagogic state, such as at the end of a meditation, or while dozing off to sleep, or the words you hear in a dream right as your alarm goes off, while driving, walking, in the shower, or if you're doing something repetitive or monotonous. So, you may connect your awareness through an experience of expanded Consciousness but it might take one of these moments to receive the insight.

We grow what we pay attention to. I recommend a dedicated journal to record your moments of intuition or pure Consciousness. You can also use it to record synchronicities, signs, omens, and any significant dreams.

What is required now is practice. But first let's reflect on any past experiences of intuition. By doing so, we bring to our awareness what it feels like to successfully experience our dimensional Consciousness, which helps us as we learn to expand it.

Recall a time when you heard your intuition. What was the exact situation? Can you describe the feeling?

_____
_____
_____
_____
_____

Did you follow your intuition at that time? Is so, what happened when you did? What was the outcome?

_____
_____
_____
_____

Exercising Our Awareness of Energy

For these next exercises, we will be focusing on our Being. If you need to, review the section on Being State in the second chapter, *The Power of a Meditation Practice*. As we begin to extend our feeling it is helpful to treat your attempt as playful, don't take it too seriously; take on an exploratory mind frame, and have fun as you discover this new sense.

A good place to start exercising an awareness of energy is in nature, whether in a park, the forest, or the beach. Each environment contains a subtle, ethereal energy that permeates the landscape.

While in your natural environment of choice, bring your focus to your Being. Try "feeling" your environment with your Being.

What did you notice? Did anything come to mind? If nothing occurred, just write what you experienced.

_____
_____

Have you ever walked into a room filled with people, maybe a funeral or a work meeting, and the "vibe" was heavy. For every space you're in with others, we form a collective Consciousness that one can feel. The next time you enter a room outside your home, focus on your Being and try "feeling" the collective Consciousness of the environment.

What did you notice? Did anything come to mind? If nothing occurred, just write what you experienced.

_____
_____

We are always feeling other people's energy, most often unconsciously. It can be helpful to think about connecting with other people as resonant vibrations of energy. When we are around someone who makes us feel good, we are resonating with their energy, while being drained by someone is when their energy is out of resonance with us.

The next time you interact with someone, preferably a stranger, or someone you don't interact with regularly (as sometimes we can be stuck in patterns of behaviors with those whom we are familiar with, which can make it difficult to listen to ourselves), bring your awareness to your Being, and focus on this other, trying to feel them in your heart. Can you feel their "vibe," their mood, or their energy? What did you notice doing this? Did anything come to mind?

_____
_____

If doing any of these exercises makes you feel drained, try repeating a proclamation, have a quick power meditation, or draw a circle of light around you to reground your energy. Sometimes after extending our "feeling" it is helpful to reground ourselves, especially if it's with a person's energy that we don't want to absorb. It's good to have an open heart, but we want to be conscious of touching another's energy when we don't want to take it on. Before we move forward, now would be the perfect time to quickly have a section on protecting our energy.

Protecting our Energy

While consciously opening ourselves to the energetic world around us it is wise to learn how to protect ourselves, especially when we are reading or feeling other people's energy, as it can negatively affect us if we are not careful.

It requires a degree of conscious control to stay in our own energy and not be affected by someone else's. We gain that control by coming back to our Being, our Source. As we will learn a little later, the more we embody the Higher Self the stronger our own energy becomes, and the more we understand how to consciously control it.

A good method of protecting your energy in the moment is by focusing on the outer edge of your energy field, and draw a circle in your imagination, and then wrap a white light around this circle.

There are also some practices you can partake in to protect or cleanse your energy, such as; burning sage brush (as a method of clearing the vibration from a space), drinking a small glass of turmeric water ((1 teaspoon of ground turmeric and a glass of water, then stir) which is healing for the body and produces a calming effect in your energy), before you sit on a public seat draw an X with your finger on it to erase the residual energy from others, (other people's energy, especially from the base of their spine, can linger there and you can absorb it if you're not careful), and avoid people touching your spine (whether with hugs or pats on the back, as your energy system runs through it and we can accidentally be affected by their energy if they touch it).

There are also objects you can keep in your vicinity to protect or cleanse your energy, such as; Himalayan rock salt (which emits a soothing vibration), flowing or running water (which releases negative ions, the healing properties of nature), and blessed objects have a special and protective vibration (such as Malas).

Plenty of these may sound hokey but after you gain an experience of feeling the energy of an environment, or from others, you will notice the above methods will be grounding and protective. All of these I can personally attest to.

Exercising Our Awareness of Energy with the Dream Self

If the last exercise to experience our state of energy didn't work for you, no problem, different modalities work with different people. Here we attempt again, but this time we bring in the dream self, because deep inside the subconscious is the voice of our pure Consciousness - our intuitive self.

Remember our exercises in the last chapter when we opened ourselves to the subconscious mind through dreams and active imagination. Bring to mind anything you experienced from those exercises. Maybe it was a dream you analyzed, or a discovery of subconscious content from active imagination. Take a moment to ponder the "feeling" of accessing content from your subconscious. Maybe you can draw on a sensation or orientation in your mind. Ponder this for a second. Do your best here as this may take some practice to get used to. We will call this identifying with the 'dream state.'

Again, choose an environment or object in nature and begin feeling it with your Being. As soon as you have a moment of connection, close your eyes, come to your dream state, and see what subconscious image comes up for yourself. Just release yourself to your first impression. Trust the feeling of your first imprint and see how your subconscious interprets it.

What did you notice? Did anything come to mind?

_____

_____

_____

The next time you enter a room with people outside your home, focus on your Being and try "feeling" the collective consciousness of the environment. As soon as you feel the space, close your eyes, come to your dream state, and see what subconscious image is produced. Just release yourself to your first impression. Trust the feeling of your first imprint and see how your subconscious interprets it.

What did you notice? Did anything come to mind?

_____

_____

_____

The next time you interact with someone, preferably a stranger, bring your awareness to your Being, and try to feel them in your heart. While you engage them, come to your dream state, and try to observe if any subconscious images are produced in your mind's eye. Just release yourself to your first impression. Trust the feeling of your first imprint and see how your subconscious interprets it.

What did you experience? Did you notice if any colours come to mind?

_____

_____

_____

Don't forget to draw a circle of light around you if you feel you need to protect your energy.

Exercising Our Awareness of Energy with Tat Tavm Asi

Our heart is an energy that knows exactly what is going on in the invisible unified world around it. In nature, in the environment of your choice, bring your focus to your Being and repeat Tat Tavm Asi in your mind or out loud, while feeling your environment.

What did you notice? Did anything come to mind?
_____
_____
_____

Upon entering a room with people, focus on your Being, repeat Tat Tavm Asi, either quietly or out loud, while feeling the collective Consciousness of the environment.

What did you notice? Did anything come to mind?
_____
_____
_____

The next time you interact with someone, preferably a stranger, bring your awareness to your Being, and try to feel them in your heart, while repeating Tat Tavm Asi privately

What did you notice? Did anything come to mind?
_____
_____
_____

If any of these exercises worked for you that's great, if not, no problem, as we will continue with exercises to expand your awareness of your dimensionality and of your Source. Come back to these basic exercises which bring awareness to our energy as they will eventually work for you. It's often just the right modality or explanation that's required to open us up to our energy.

Opening Ourselves to Dimensionality

There is No Space

We established earlier that a property of quantum reality states that the Universe exists in no space, and that Consciousness originates here, this being the Absolute. We have access to "no space" because any point of the Universe is available to us, without distance being an issue, as long as we know how to bring that local to our focus.

The conscious mind, with its typical mental noise, such as memory, imagination, and normal thoughts about its day, prevent us from experiencing this ability of Consciousness. But when the desire is there, we can see things in other places. These steps are a helpful guide to see things regardless of distance.

1. Belief

It starts with belief. Believing in this ability reinforces the positive outcome of the experience. You have to know you are connected to everything. Believe in yourself and know with certainty by saying out loud;

I can see anything I want to.

If the motivation is there, you will be able to see beyond space to another local.

2. Choosing a Location

The second step is to have a goal, something you desire to see. It can be anything that is imaginable; events, places, objects, people, functions, etc.

We are connected to everything, and love is the frequency, therefore as we begin, we will experience a greater ease of sight to that which we love. You can see how a loved one is doing, or check in on the well-being of a friend, but you can also use it for mundane things for yourself, such as where to find a parking spot at the mall. Importantly, choose a target in which you can receive feedback regarding your success.

Whatever you choose the intention needs to be real. You have to have a target with your Being, with your heart, not with your mind. You can make this work when the intention is pure, and not driven to prove something or make one feel special.

Say it out loud or write here what you want to see.

_____

_____

If you are having trouble finding a location but still with an innocent heart want to practice this ability, then go to a spot in a city you are unfamiliar with, find a bench, and then with the steps below "see" what is around the corner.

3. Moving the Mind Out of the Way

If you need to, revisit the section on meditation, dreams, and active imagination. One needs to be able to move one's mind from the focus of the outer world to an open subconscious state. We want to bypass the analytical mind and clear our thoughts of judgments and assumptions.

If your mind is distracted or cluttered you can try writing down what you are thinking about, or anything that concerns you, on a piece of paper and then throw it away. Or you can make a note on your smartphone, and then delete it. By doing so, we symbolically eliminate the mental disturbance for a brief period, to provide the full attention to the exercise at hand.

Relax your mind and Being, clearing any thoughts you have.

4. Refrain From Attempting to See

Do not attempt to see the location yet as you need to artificially stimulate a response procedure, by doing so the subconscious responds to the intention. Choose a neutral word such as "see" to tell your mind (though you can choose any that suits you). This allows us to focus on a moment before the mind forms ideas, first impressions, or concepts.

5. It Starts With a Glimpse

Now, with the desired target declared, say to yourself "see," and focus on your first impression of the local.

The window through the noise of the mind, with which to accurately see something, is .5 to 1 second. Any information you get, for the time being, just consider it correct. Don't speculate. If you get another image or feeling after the first, you can trust this.

But when the same image or feeling repeats, then you have to be more careful, as this increases the likelihood that you are dealing with imagination, or memory.

If you did not receive a first impression of feeling or imagery, no problem, but stop trying. Take a break first and clear your mind, then try again.

6. Refrain From Full Pictures

Make note of your first impression, feeling or imagery, and freeze it in your mind, either mentally or by writing it down. Just allow for a fleeting bit, so much that it should be vague, and abstract. Refrain from trying to recover full pictures, and if you do, discard them.

If you're drawing what you see, again refrain from interpreting, make simple strokes on a page, such as a line, curve, single word, or symbol, whatever works in getting a minimum first impression. Resist letting the mind fill it in.

7. Take a Break

Then take a break to relax. It can be as brief as a few seconds, or as long as several minutes, whatever is needed to completely remove yourself from thinking about the process of seeing the target. We want to think about the object of focus on short durations, with multiple first impressions. This is for the purpose of curtailing any potential thoughts that try to fill in the gaps of the image seen.

8. Repeat

Using the same procedure, continue and repeat, focusing on different details, such as the textures, colours, and function of what you're looking at.

Correct pictures will be built from multiple smaller glimpses, gradually assembled into one large image.

It is important to eventually receive feedback about your location of choice, to gain confidence in your ability. You can call up the person you looked at, and ask them about their environment, or you can do it in a location in which you can access.

The more you practice this ability, like exercising a muscle at the gym, the easier it will become in identifying true images and feelings that come from another space. It will help if you continue, several times a day, switching up the types of targets or locations.

There is No Time

Time, as we all know, is a measure of events, while space is the continuum that contains them. Time by its nature acts as a flow, but at the source of the Universe all time, or no time, is available to us, just like no space, as long as we know how to focus on it.

The idea that we have access to other moments on our timeline is very foreign to humans and this is because we are used to the flow of time in one direction. But we don't just have access to our past and future, but also beyond our current physical manifestation, into past and future lives. Adding to the complexities is that we also deal with probabilities, as the present moment actions can create varying outcomes that we can influence consciously, which is the practice of Visioning, something we will get into later.

With no time you are able to see future events, know the outcomes of life choices, and also have past life awareness, all at your fingertips, all of which we will explore here.

Discovering Your Past Life

And this true identity has a long history of many manifestations and forms you would call lives. | Your true individual histories spans other places, other galaxies, other times, and other dimensions.
-*The Mystic Book*

Past lives are real, we all have them, and many people are aware of their own past lives, and many who are not can still feel that they have been living for a lot longer than this life. They can be fascinating to uncover, but it can also be a very helpful method of self-discovery to understand the origin of our tendencies, and how the imprints left from previous lives affect your present life.

Past lives are accessed both through the Higher Self existing in no time, which can provide visions ripe with present moment experiences (such as sensations, weather, and mind frame of the past life), but are also accessed through the memories stored in the mind of the ethereal body, which has evolved over time through the birth and death life cycle.

1. Belief

The same with the last exercise, when we attempted to see any location we desired, it starts with belief. Your ability to believe that you have past lives reinforces the positive outcome of discovering them. You have to know that you existed in many lives before this one, even if at present you can't conceive of them. Believe and know with certainty by saying out loud;

I can see any of my past lives that I want to.

If the motivation is there, you will be able to see the lives of your recurring Self.

2. Discovering Our Connection to a Past Life

The second step is to have a goal, something you want to see, and for a past life it can come from several different desires.

We all have a historical period that intrigues us, or that we have been attracted to, and there is a reason for that. Often, we find ourselves interested in a historical period when the life we lived at that time provided positive feelings; maybe we were in love, were happy, or had purpose. We come back to that life subconsciously, out of the attraction for who we were and what we had at that time. Or maybe you have glimpsed the feeling that you have engaged in an activity, action, or behaviour which is foreign to you in this life, such as driving a bomber plane, owning slaves, or living in the desert.

Or maybe you haven't experienced any of the above but are intrigued by a behaviour, habit, or hobby you do, but can't quite understand why you do it. It's possible it's created from a tendency built from a past life. Or maybe you gravitate towards a certain type of people in your life, have an unexplained fascination, or have a friend, a loved one, family member, or an acquaintance, whose connection feels like it originates from another life and you want to understand it.

Make any one of the above your focus.

Whatever you choose the intention for discovery needs to be real. You have to have a target with your Being and your heart, not with your mind. You can make this work when the intention is pure, and not driven to prove something or make one feel special.

Say it out loud or write here what you want to see.

---

3. Preparing Ourselves for Past Life Awareness

It's very common to assume gaining past life awareness is similar to remembering the past of our current life. For example, take a moment to recall anything from when you were sixteen years old, maybe you can remember your sixteenth birthday, or your favourite pop artist. This is not where past lives live; they are not brought up in the memory of the brain but are experienced the way you experience your present life - living in the now. Past life memories are present moment experiences for that life, and this is because time is an illusion. We live in timelessness and all those lives we have are Being experienced right now. Only your Consciousness is real, and it lives in timelessness. This is where your true Being is.

Past lives are another life lived with the same heart you have now, but often surrounded by very different circumstances. To discover those circumstances, we have to be completely open to let them take shape, dropping our ideals and expectations. You don't go living the same type of life over and over again. You're living out your tendencies but often within very different circumstances or contexts; maybe you were the opposite sex and don't expect it, maybe you were a personality type you don't expect, maybe you were in a position in society you don't expect, maybe you were a race you don't expect.

4. Moving the Mind Out of the Way

As mentioned in the previous exercise, if you need to, revisit the section on meditation, dreams, and active imagination. One needs to be able to move the mind from the focus of the outer world and be receptive to a subconscious state. We want to bypass the analytical mind and clear our thoughts of judgments and assumptions.

If your mind is distracted or cluttered you can try writing down what you are thinking about, or anything that concerns you, on a piece of paper and then throw it away. Or you can make a note on your smartphone, and then delete it. By doing so, we symbolically eliminate the mental disturbance for a brief period, to provide the full attention to the exercise at hand.

Relax your mind and Being, clearing any thoughts you have.

There are multiple ways to gain past life awareness. You could program your subconscious to show you with a dream of your past life and see what it provides.

Simply state before you fall asleep;

Subconscious, show me my past life through a dream.

Hypnotic regression is an effective method at gaining past life awareness, therefore you could visit a licensed hypnotherapist, which I recommend if you're concerned about exposing traumatic memories. Otherwise for simple self-exploration you could conduct a self-hypnosis meditation.

Set yourself up to audio record yourself, such as on a smartphone. Using the meditation posture, close your eyes, and conduct a normal five-minute meditation as laid out in the previous section of this book to relax yourself. Then when your ready command your subconscious;

When I count down to twenty, I am going to see my past life.

Begin slowly counting down to twenty, with each number imagine you are taking a step down a stair, going deeper into your subconscious. Then begin speaking whatever you experience. When you feel ready, come out of the regression slowly, taking a few deep breaths.

You can also try the same method as we used in the last exercise to receive glimpses of other locations, by using the following steps.

5. Refrain From Attempting to See the Past Life

Do not attempt to see the past life yet as you need to artificially stimulate a response procedure, by doing so the subconscious responds to the intention. Choose a neutral word such as "see" to tell your mind (though you can choose any that suits you). This allows us to focus on a moment before the mind forms ideas, first impressions, or concepts.

6. It Starts With a Glimpse

Now, with the desired past life target, say to yourself "see," and focus on your first impression.

The window through the noise of the mind, with which to accurately see something, is .5 to 1 second. Any information you get, for the time being, just consider it correct. Don't speculate. If you get another image or feeling after the first, you can trust this.

But when the same image or feeling repeats, then you have to be more careful, as this increases the likelihood that you're dealing with imagination, or present memory.

If you did not receive a first impression of feeling or imagery, no problem, but stop trying. Take a break first and clear your mind, then try again.

7. Refrain From Full Pictures

Make note of your first impression, feeling or imagery and freeze it in your mind, either mentally or by writing it down. Just allow for a fleeting bit, so much that it should be vague, and abstract. Refrain from trying to recover full pictures, and if you do, discard them.

If you're drawing what you see, again refrain from interpreting, by making simple strokes on a page, such as a line, curve, single word, or symbol, whatever works in getting a minimum first impression. Resist letting the mind fill it in.

8. Take a Break

Then take a break to relax. It can be as brief as a few seconds, or as long as several minutes, whatever is needed to completely remove yourself from thinking about the process of seeing the past life. We want to think about the object of focus on short durations, with multiple first impressions. This is for the purpose of curtailing any potential thoughts that try to fill in the gaps of the image seen.

9. Repeat

Using the same procedure, continue and repeat, focusing on different details of your past identity, such as relationships (spouse, mother, father, siblings, friends), occupation/purpose, spiritual/religious worldview, or community worldview/social standing. As any one of these could be similar to, or very different from, how you think of them in your present life, it can take time to put that life together. Correct pictures will be built from multiple smaller glimpses gradually assembled over time into one large narrative.

The glimpse of past life memories can vary in their type. It can be a small glimpse or a spontaneous vision accompanied by information you have never had in your conscious mind. Like peering through a window, you pick up the mental mindframe of that past self.

To use a personal example, I had a flash of a vision of an individual with an ancient worldview, when existence was harsher, accompanied by the distinct feeling of identifying as ancient Jewish - an Israelite - with an awareness of Roman occupation. This life was not my own but felt a part of me. This other me was in a conflict with someone; there was a dirt road, a ditch, we were out on farmlands, and I had a fear of being whipped. I knew that if I got whipped, I would possibly die from the infection afterwards. My present self rarely, if ever, contemplates the after-effects of being wiped. I then learned from research that Roman whips were serrated, often with blood and dirt on them from other victims. Without a doubt, a person would get an infection from being whipped, and with the lack of proper antibiotics, they would most likely die.

It is important to eventually receive feedback about the accuracy of your past life awareness, to gain confidence in your ability. With research most small details of any historical period can be found online. And if you learn of the location of your past life, Google Street View has access to images from many locations in the world.

The more you practice this ability, like exercising a muscle at the gym, the easier it will become in identifying true images and feelings that come from a past life. If you continue, switching up with different past lives, this will help.

A last tip to mention; if you come across traumatic memories in your past life, and you don't feel you need to address them with a hypnotherapist, then at this time, I recommend to not bring them up, and to just avoid these memories as best as you can. We will address past life traumas in another section in the Visioning chapter.

Making Life Choices, Sensing Outcomes, and Seeing the Future

Being told we can see the future conjures up ideas of prophets, psychics, and charlatans, but in these exercises, we are not focusing on predictions of worldwide events, or prophesying another's future, but of your own, allowing you to see that it can be done and just how accurate you can be.

We can see the future, at least the outcome of probable futures. Some things in your future are set in stone, others can be changed through Visioning. Our timelines are complex and morph with our lives, and the choices we make.

Making Life Choices

A single choice can change your life. Free will with the option to choose is the reason we live here in the physical realm; to experience choice in a world we believe to be real, while in the Absolute there is no choice to make, because all space and time outcomes are known and experienced. To choose then becomes the singular greatest creative action we can partake in while here in the physical realm.

We all face life choices; Should you go back to school to educate yourself and take time off of work? Should you date that new person? Should you take that job offer? Should you move to that new city for that new opportunity? But we also make small choices that affect our day or our relationships, such as choosing what we should do on our day off, or what gift we should get our friend.

We all simply want to know what's the right choice.

Our intuition is that part of us that knows future outcomes, therefore one method of connecting with our intuition is by being in touch with our heart and feelings in the present moment, and simply ask yourself *What do I feel like doing?*

Another method is by asking *What would be the fun thing to do?* or *Which path looks the most beautiful?* The joy of our spirit speaks through that which our heart finds fun, and the love of our spirit speaks through that which our heart finds beautiful.

Sometimes, our bodies, as its own organism, can provide us with an intuition of what choice is best for us at the very moment we have to make a decision. Say you have to make a choice whether to leave your job to educate yourself, or to stay climbing the corporate ladder. Imagine yourself the day you're telling your boss you're quitting; how does your body feel in this imagination as you tell her. Try to imagine your body responding exactly at the moment you have to make the decision. What choice does it make?

Similar to the above, there is also the method of pretending to put your choice into motion. Try stating out loud your choices and notice how your body feels as you mention them to others. Say you want to change careers, talk to people out loud and see how it feels to say it.

Reliance on Self is about paying attention and trusting our feelings, and then taking action. It is important to act on what you hear. When you do, you're giving the message to your Higher Self that you take it seriously, which solidifies your relationship with it.

Seeing the Future

1. Belief

Like the last exercise, it starts with belief. Your ability to believe you can sense the future reinforces the positive outcome of experiencing it. You have to know you are connected to all events in time, including the future. Believe in yourself and know with certainty by saying out loud;

I can feel, sense, and see anything in my future that I want to.

If the motivation is there, you will be able to see beyond this present moment into your future.

2. Choosing a Future Moment or Outcome

The second step is to have a goal, something you desire to see in the future. It can be anything that is imaginable; events, places, objects, people, functions, etc.

We are connected to everything, and love is the frequency, therefore as we begin, we will experience a greater ease of sight to that which we love. You can see how a loved one will fare, or check on the outcome of a friend's choice, or you can use it for yourself seeing how a future event will turn out.

If you want to see the possible outcomes of different choices, draw several lines out on a piece of paper, as if it is an organizational chart, like they are options on a timeline.

Whatever you choose the intention needs to be real. You have to have a target with your Being, with your heart, not with your mind. You can make this work when the intention is pure, and not driven to prove something or make one feel special.

Say out loud or write here, either the outcome you would like to know, the outcome of several different choices, or the future event you would like to see.

3. Moving the Mind Out of the Way

If you need to, revisit the section on meditation, dreams, and active imagination. One needs to be able to move one's mind from the focus of the outer world to an open subconscious state. We want to bypass the analytical mind and clear our thoughts of judgments and assumptions.

If your mind is distracted or cluttered you can try writing down what you are thinking about on a piece of paper and then throw it away. Or you can make a note on your smartphone, and then delete it. By doing so, we symbolically eliminate the mental disturbance for a brief period, to provide our full attention to the exercise at hand.

Relax your mind and Being, clearing any thoughts you have.

4. Refrain From Attempting to See

Do not attempt to see the future event yet as you need to artificially stimulate a response procedure, by doing so the subconscious responds to the intention. Choose a neutral word such as "see" to tell your mind (though you can choose any that suits you). This allows us to focus on a moment before the mind forms ideas, first impressions, or concepts.

5. It Starts With a Glimpse

Now, with the desired target declared, say to yourself "see," and focus on your first impression.

If you're choosing a specific event in the future, you could place your finger over the date on a calendar, say to yourself "see," and focus on your first impression.

If you're looking at multiple outcomes on a timeline, place your finger at the end of each drawn line, one at a time, saying to yourself "see," and focus on your first impression.

The window through the noise of the mind, with which to accurately see something, is .5 to 1 second. Any information you get, for the time being, just consider it correct. Don't speculate. If you get another image or feeling after the first, you can trust this. But when the same image or feeling repeats, then you have to be more careful, as this increases the likelihood that you are dealing with imagination, or memory.

If you did not receive a first impression of feeling or imagery, no problem, but stop trying. Take a break first and clear your mind, then try again.

6. Refrain From Full Pictures

Make note of your first impression, feeling or imagery and freeze it in your mind, either mentally or by writing it down. Just allow for a fleeting bit, so much that it should be vague, and abstract. Refrain from trying to recover full pictures, and if you do, discard them.

If you're drawing what you see, again refrain from interpreting by making simple strokes on a page, such as a line, curve, single word, or symbol, whatever works in getting a minimum first impression. Just resist letting the mind fill it in.

7. Take a Break

Then take a break to relax. It can be as brief as a few seconds, or as long as several minutes, whatever is needed to completely remove yourself from thinking about the process of seeing the future outcome. We want to think about the object of focus in short durations, with multiple first impressions. This is for the purpose of curtailing any potential thoughts that try to fill in the gaps of the image seen.

8. Repeat

Using the same procedure, continue and repeat, focusing on different details, such as the location, and people involved. Correct pictures will be built from multiple smaller glimpses, gradually assembled into one large image.

It is important to eventually receive feedback to gain confidence in your ability. Eventually you will find out if your future event or outcome was as you saw it, which will help you know your accuracy.

The more you practice this ability, like exercising a muscle at the gym, the easier it will become in identifying true images and feelings that are impressions of the future.

Summary

Were you successful at experiencing any of the above exercises? If you were, take a second to reflect on how it makes you feel that you were successful, and what you think it means for you. Write here what you came up with.

_____
_____
_____

You had a glimpse of your true nature, as a no space and no time Consciousness, and the unlimited potential that you have. You are a magnificent being and we are just getting started.

If you were unable to experience your timelessness and spacelessness, no problem; try coming back to this section after The Rising chapter, as awakening ourselves to our Source can better allow us to experience our dimensionality.

Knowing our Source is within us is the beginning of understanding this next proclamation meditation.

The Third Proclamation

The Source is within you - the known power of the Universe resides inside. The purpose of the third proclamation is to experience that Source, God, resides within, and that you are connected to it.

I introduce an ancient Sanskrit dictum as the third proclamation; **Ayam Atman Brahman** (Source: Atharvaveda, Mandukya Upanisad 1.2)

Phonetically it is;

Ah-yam At-ma Brahm-ha

Ayam means My, *Atman* means Consciousness, and *Brahman* means Creator. Therefore, the meaning of this proclamation is <u>My Consciousness is the Creator</u>.

My teacher would repeat the aphorism, "As the Universe so the Individual and as the Individual so the Universe; As the Macrocosm so the Microcosm and as the Microcosm so the Macrocosm."

This proclamation imbues the meditator with the relationship of Consciousness to Universal Consciousness, that the Creator is within, yet their individuation remains.

Repeat this Proclamation in your meditation by breathing in through your nose and on your exhale, say Ahyam Atma Brahma by elongating the vowels; not too slow and not too fast.

As my teacher says; *"It is through you the Universe continues its creation by becoming you."*

In each of us is the permanence, the stillness of our Self, and this permanent Self is the Atman, is Consciousness.

Your Consciousness is the Creator. Your Being is God, is Source, is the power of the Universe, just as the tree is to the leaf, or ocean to the wave of the ocean, or flame to the spark of the flame. The spark and the flame are identical, as the spark has all the power of the flame to start a new fire. We are God-lets, living out our existence within, as, and with Source, with all the same power to create our own Universe.

Sit and reflect that God, the Source of the Universe, is within you. What does it mean to you? How does it feel to be told this? Write your answer below.

_____
_____
_____
_____
_____
_____
_____

Detachment

Eventually, in the search for spirit, you have to come face to face with yourself, it's where your Source is. Yet, when our world is filled with distractions, the power within us can't be fully utilized; this is why we learn detachment.

Detachment is best thought of as the conservation of our personal psychological energy. Everything you give yourself to in your world takes your psychological energy; your job, your family, etc. And when we have no sense of our true identity as Source within, we form mental habits, which are grooves of neurons formed in the brain, that let the external people, objects, and actions define us.

Without exploring detachment eventually you will hit a barrier to your own spiritual development, to your own Rising. Progress will not be made. It is with detachment that we maintain a connection to our higher spiritual awareness in our world, while conducting our daily activities.

Honestly, only with detachment can we ever truly find peace, happiness, and fulfillment. Detachment allows us to accept the complications and hardships of life and allows us to be open to all situations. It is how we begin to open ourselves to the larger Universe within us, and this is because your Higher Self, the conscious unified field force itself, exists in a detached state from our concerns and emotional issues.

Coming Face to Face With Yourself

You seek something you don't know you seek.

When we come to spirituality, we have an unconscious desire for a paradigm shift, to experience a grander version of ourselves.

Yet the only way to achieve that is through the ontological shock of full detachment from your life, so much so that all that is left is you - just you. Full detachment is the feeling of completely abandoning your life - just walking out the door - removing yourself from everything that defines you, and coming face to face with yourself. But in fact, what you find is your Creator, the God that all along has been within. Extreme detachment is the only way through the door of your enlightenment. It is the fulfillment we seek, yet lack within, and so we project out and seek it externally.

Many seek this extreme detachment by changing their environment and associations, such as I did when I fulfilled the messages of the Rising.

Joseph Campbell identified it as the hero's journey, in which the hero, in response to a call to adventure, removes themselves from their typical environment, which creates a transformative revelation symbolized as a death and rebirth.

And there are many rituals that seek to emulate this removal, such as the Australian aboriginal Walkabout which is a rite of passage where young males take a journey into the wilderness, living alone off of the land for up to six months. Or in Hinduism when a Sannyasin moves into an ashram to renounce themselves of attachments and the demands of the world around them, which is also similar to Christian monks who renounce the world to live in a monastery.

Doing any of these destroys old mental patterns, habits, and dependencies which typically dissipate our energy, and keep our Consciousness fixed on the physical level.

What peers through is the unspeakable Self, the light, the Source. And the practice one applies at this point trains the mind to become steady with God. From this proceeds an awakening to the super dimensions of Consciousness, the pure awareness that is untouched by time, space, and causation.

Atman is Existence, it is Real, it is bhāva which means awareness or pure consciousness. Awareness remains untouched by time, space, and causation.
  -Swami Chidbavanunda, commentary on the Bhagavad Gita

Though most of us desire security and consistency, we unconsciously long for the shock of extreme detachment because, from what I learned in the white room, we all seek to discover ourselves as an orb within; a collapsed energy form, self-sufficient, self-reliant, and in full Unity with our Source - a Unity where all that matters is that Unity. Words like detachment don't even exist there because there is no conceivable reality that takes you away from your inherent, natural, truthful, connection to the Universe. This is the space where you know for certain that the Source's desire is your desire, and your desire is its desire.

So instead, we unconsciously project this desire by going on vacations, camping trips, or retreats, all in an attempt to gain a glimpse of that extreme detachment - to experience a Self independent from the things around us which we have used to define us

I Am Exercise

You seem to have lost your original identity and have identified with your thoughts and body. Suppose I ask you who you are. If you say, "I am a man," you have identified yourself with a masculine body. If you say, "I am a professor," you are identifying with the ideas gathered in your brain. If you say, "I am a millionaire," you are identifying with your bank account; if "a mother," with a child, "a husband," with a wife. "I am tall; I am short, I am black or white" shows your identification with the shape and color of the body. But without any identifications, who are you? Have you ever thought about it? When you really understand that you will see we are all the same. If you detach yourself completely from all the things you have identified yourself with, you realize yourself as the pure "I." In that pure "I" there is no difference between you and me.
  -Swami Satchidananda, Commentary on the Yoga Sutras of Patanjali

On a piece of loose 8 ½ by 11 white paper, such as printing paper, draw a medium sized circle in the center, roughly 2 inches in diameter. Then draw a large circle with a diameter that reaches the edge of the page with the smaller circle centered in the middle. In the center circle write "I am."

Then, like a pie chart, draw lines, not penetrating the center but, starting at the circumference of the center circle, and radiating to the circumference of the outer circle.

In each of the pies, you are going to write your I am, such as "...a spouse," "...an accountant," "...a business partner." Make as many as necessary. Put in everything you identify yourself as including labels, such as "...creative," "...an introvert," "...a male," "...tall." Fill in as many pie slices as you can think of.

Now look at this diagram and notice that your I am is separate from every label you gave yourself.

Take a pair of scissors, fold the paper in half and cut out the I am in the center. Then hold the I am circle in your hands. Look at it. Feel this is your I am. Look back at the diagram now with an empty hole where your I am was.

For the time being, put the pie chart away and hold onto the I am.

I Am Meditation

As you place yourself for meditation leave your 'I am circle' directly in front of you, so that it will be easy to reach in a meditative state.

Close your eyes and take a breath through your nose and into your diaphragm as you normally would for your meditation. Just sit here for a second while you focus on your breathing.

Now ask out loud, "Who created me?" Say "I." Repeat several times, "I, I, I, I." Again ask, "Who created me? Say and repeat, "I, I, I, I." Again ask, "Who created me? Say and repeat, "I, I, I, I."

Now still in meditation, take hold of your 'I am circle,' and repeat "I am, I am, I am." As you do, remember the pie slices on your paper, all your identities, and how right now, in your hand, you hold your I am. You are separate from those labels.

Still holding the 'I am circle' in your hand we are now going to go into a visualization. Before we do, take a few deep breaths.

In this visualization you are going to leave your life. However you want, imagine that you have received what you would consider to be a divine message, a message from Source, to leave your life. Maybe it was through the words in a book you resonated with, maybe it was a moment of divine sight, maybe it was through a dream. This message told you to leave your life and take a leap of faith. To leave your life to find yourself, to find God within. As inconceivable as this is, in the moment this message feels right. All of your family, though they will miss you, have accepted your journey of the heart. If you have children who depend on you, imagine just for this visualization that out of nowhere, someone you trust is willing to take care of them and let you live your journey. Take a moment to imagine this.

Now, you have left your life. It has been a few weeks and you have learned to take care of yourself. In this moment you are walking deep in nature, with no sign of mankind - isolated and remote. Day in and day out, walking through endless forests. All you have is a backpack, your basic necessities are all with you, but you left behind your identity. It's just you. Though you may be on edge, you feel guided to do this and therefore know you are safe. Take a moment to imagine this wondering.

Now, it's getting dark and you set up your camp along a lake. You set up your tent, a fire, and your dinner. It's now nighttime, with the alone, black, dark lake in front of you. With your campfire extinguished, you set up to meditate on a rock overlooking the dark lake. The clear night sky with bright stars are out but no moon. The forest is quiet, black, and the air is warm. You are alone but feel safe.

It's just you, the sky, and nature. You are alone, and isolated. See the darkness in nature surrounding you. Pure black.

Now recall your 'I am circle.' Recall how even though you had made a lot of identities in your previous life, your I am was separate, that I am which you are face to face with now, here alone and isolated out in the wilderness.

Now begin repeating "I am" out loud in your meditation. As you do, see the darkness surrounding you in nature. Maybe you can glimpse a connection with the nature around you as you repeat "I am," with the quiet dark forest, the calm lake, or the expansive star-filled sky.

You are face to face with yourself.

Say "Ayam Atma Brahman - My Consciousness is the Creator," three times.

Even though you are alone, isolated, and deep in the wilderness from all humans, your Consciousness is the Creator means something very important:

You Are Not Alone.

You are face to face with yourself. But you are not alone.
You are isolated in the wilderness surrounded by darkness. But you are not alone.
Ayam Atma Brahman. Your Consciousness is the Creator.

Repeat Ayam Atma Brahman out loud for a length of time that feels comfortable.

When you're done, sit with this feeling. Sit with your Consciousness, with the realization that the conscious unified field force is within, and you are not alone. Breath into this truth.

Your journey of removing yourself from society has been long and arduous, but now you feel it is time to come back. And you are bringing back that connection you experienced, what you came face to face with within, that sense of Self that you touched.

Imagine your family embracing you as you see yourself coming back to society.

Take one last breath and slowly come out of this meditation and come back into the world.

End this exercise by placing your 'I am circle' back into the center of the pie chart. Take a moment to reflect on what that feels like.

How did it feel to do this exercise? What did you discover?

If you were still in this visualization would you come back to the same life that you have now?

We don't have to leave our lives, our loved ones, or what we love to do, but the experience of removal gives us grounding to make a vision of detachment for our lives, especially from those habits that we know inhibit us from experiencing our higher Consciousness.

A Vision of Non-Attachment

Non-attachment should not be misunderstood to be indifference. Vairagya (non-attachment) literally means "colorless." Vi is "without," raga is "color." Every desire brings its own color to the mind. The moment you color the mind, a ripple is formed just as when a stone is thrown into a calm lake, it creates waves in the water. When the mind is tossed by these desires one after the other, there won't be peace or rest in the mind. And with a restless mind you can't have steady practice. When you want to do something constantly, your mind should not be distracted by other desires. That's why this sort of dispassion or non-attachment must always go with the practice. Any practice without this non- attachment can never be fulfilled.
-Swami Satchidananda, Commentary on the Yoga Sutras of Patanjali

Our habits form neural grooves in our brain, which are treated as a single conglomerate of circuitry allowing us to act automatically; such as with driving our car or brushing our teeth. But we also do this with more subtle thoughts and behaviors such as, needing to drink alcohol when we have experienced hard or heavy emotions, or looking at shocking things on the internet to stave off boredom.

The brain is designed to act automatically so valuable neural energy isn't overtaxed focusing on the minute details of our activities. The result is habits can be hard to break, especially our attachments, or those that were created to suppress complex or challenging emotions. Therefore, it is of the utmost importance to be gentle with yourself as we attempt to detach from those things that inhibit us.

I recommend not being dogmatic in your approach to your attachments, and to cultivate a neutral stance to observe the thoughts in your mind, and the sensations in your body. It might be helpful then to review the sections in the previous chapters; *Observing our Thoughts*, *The Power of the Observer Self*, and *Stepping Back from Thoughts*.

Which of your habits are attachments? Only you can know for yourself but there is an exercise provided to help you discern.

Recall in the previous chapters, *Our Inner Architecture: Discerning the Voice of the Mind and the Voice of the Heart* and *Discerning the Voices of the Heart and Mind Through Intentions of Love and Fear*, where we explored intentions and learned how to distinguish those that originated in the heart versus our mind, and those that proceeded from love versus fear. Here we are going to expand on those exercises to discover the intentions of those things that take up your daily life. Again, feel free to review those sections if needed.

List three habits you partake in during the morning, aside from those that help get you ready for the day. For example, scrolling through social media, or going for a morning run.

1. _____

2. _____

3. _____

List three habits you partake in at work, aside from those that help in your responsibilities. For example, grabbing a cup of coffee, or having a midday sweet treat.

1. _____

2. _____

3. _____

List three habits you partake in after you get home from work, aside from those that are required such as making dinner. For example, zoning out watching TV, or having a glass of wine.

1. _____

2. _____

3. _____

List three habits you partake in on a day off from work, aside from those that are necessary such as grocery shopping. For example, doing housework, or going to a coffee shop.

1. _____

2. _____

3. _____

    Now look back at each habit you wrote down and this time, for each one, ask yourself if the intention comes from your heart or your mind and/or from love or from fear. Write down the answer beside each. If you have trouble discerning, close your eyes, and state out loud, "This habit of (fill in the blank) is an intention of love," while observing the sensations in your body.

Your body will indicate to you through the type of sensations you experience the truth of your statement. For example, if your heart clenches slightly as you make the statement, it is likely rooted in fear. If you are calm and relaxed while you make the statement, it is likely rooted in love.

If the intention of your habit roots itself in fear, or in the mind, it is an attachment.

Try not to judge yourself. Having an attachment is not a righteous moral issue with which to create generalizations about ourselves, such as believing it means you are weak. It is simply what it is, an attachment. Have acceptance, kindness, and compassion for yourself, and again try not to judge yourself.

Now list here what you would consider to be your top five attachments. Write them in order of what you believe to be your greatest attachment as number one, through to number five.

1. _____

2. _____

3. _____

4. _____

5. _____

Now make a plan, to slightly reduce only attachment number five. For example, let's say the attachment is smoking and you smoke five cigarettes a day. Begin smoking four cigarettes a day, and no less. If the attachment is coffee and you have a large cup of coffee a day, begin to make it a medium. If the attachment is a glass of wine every day after work, now make it only after four workdays.

Choose only one attachment for the time being to get your mind used to the reduction. With the other four attachments, you're as free to be as attached as you need. For the time being we are looking to gain a sense of self reliance, but not create a mind frame that is repressive.

Then over time, observe how your mind handles the reduction. If you have any anxiety, or a craving for your attachment; just observe it. Repeat the proclamation Ayam Atma Brahman. Feel you are Consciousness. Breath into the anxiety. Maybe you have thoughts of resisting the reduction; just observe it.

Your mind might want to overcompensate with the other attachments with which you are free with. For example, if you've reduced your smoking to three cigarettes a day, your mind might anxiously want to have an extra-large coffee, as if out of rebellion, then let it (obviously with common sense, without harming your health, or adversely affecting your life in any way).

Once the mind begins to realize that the reduction was small, and that some form of it still exists, the craving for it will dissipate.

Our attachments were created for a reason so if something comes up for you, an emotional issue that it was covering up, try your best to observe it with no judgment, and seek to understand it. If you see something with which you don't like about yourself - forgive.

The pace of reduction for your attachment is now up to you, but I recommend taking your time - this is a weeks-long exercise.

When something occurs in your life, such as a success, maybe a realization you need to control yourself more, or maybe a moment when you realize you need more spiritual power, reduce one of your attachments; now to three cigarettes, or to a small cup of coffee, or to a glass of wine after only three workdays, while beginning to reduce another attachment on your list.

What this does is, though you still might be having attachments, you are not creating a repressive mind frame, while making space for a vision of your detachment by slowly committing to the reduction. Just beginning this process and committing to it will give you back the psychological energy your attachment takes away from you. You will notice the difference.

This type of pace will actually make reducing your attachments enjoyable, and maybe even exciting.

In time, the end game is complete removal of the need for your attachments.

When you are successfully detached you will experience more energy, more peace, feel more sensitive, your Being will have more power, and you may even feel a background sense of love.

The Root Cause of an Attachment

During this process of detaching, it could be helpful to understand exactly what is the root cause of your attachment, if you are not already aware. If our attachments originate from thoughts and feelings made decades ago, the origins may be obscure to us.

Simply looking at the root cause of our attachment, the thoughts and emotions that created it, can help dissipate the desire.

"What you resist persists, what you look at disappears."
   -Conversations with God

Try the *Ocean of the Mind* technique to look at the root cause of your attachment. With a specific attachment in mind, take time now to go to that exercise. Again, if you discover something that is hard to look at, forgive yourself and be compassionate.

After you completed that exercise, write here what you found.

_____
_____
_____
_____
_____
_____

There Is No Attachment When All Is Source

The detachment of the mind from its personal desires and enjoyment is the ordinary vairagya (non-attachment). The mind might want something; but, having control, you tell the mind, "No," and it stays away. But in the higher non-attachment you don't even think of attaching yourself. In other words, with the ordinary vairagya you may be completely free from new things coming in to tempt you. But what will you do with the impressions that are already in your mind? The memory of having experienced something will still be there. For example, after many years of thievery, a robber decides not to steal any more. But still, the memory of having stolen so many things and enjoyed them remains in that robber's mind. In the Yogic term these memories are called "impressions," or samskaras. Now and then the samskaras will come up: "Oh, how nice it would be if I had just stolen that car. How I would have enjoyed it. But these people came and told me not to attach myself, and I accepted it and am staying away from this." Or "I remember how much I enjoyed smoking and drinking. This Yoga business came in, and somehow I don't have those joys anymore." Many people feel like that because the samskaras are still there.

You can't just go into the mind and erase the impressions. But they get themselves erased at one point. When? When you succeed in going within and realizing the peace and joy of your own Self. The moment you understand yourself as the true Self, you find such peace and bliss that the impressions of the petty enjoyments you experienced before become as ordinary specks of light in front of the brilliant sun. You lose all interest in them permanently. That is the highest non-attachment.
  -Swami Satchidananda, Commentary on the Yoga Sutras of Patanjali

Having the love and devotion to your Source is the key to detachment. It is total one-pointed self-reliance that Consciousness is everything and provides everything. The mind has to be focused that you are God, but we can't do that when we are attached. Why? Because God is not attached. God is all things so there is nothing for it to attach to. It is the mind which thinks it is limited in the physical which gets attached.

Body Identification Exercise

Our body is our tool to create cause and effect within space and time, but we are not it. Not identifying with our bodies opens our minds to discover our Consciousness.

Think about what it means that you are not your body. How many of your day-to-day choices are because you think you are your body? Would you make different decisions regarding your job, marriage, hobbies, or lifestyle?

Identification is a psychological process termed by Sigmond Freud in which we assimilate the properties of an object into oneself, such as, buying the type of car that suits your personality. This is what most, if not all of us, have done with our body, therefore it can be helpful to use conscious methods to remove our identification.

Typically, we might say I'm hungry, I'm tired, or I'm sore. See how you feel when you try using language that removes your identity with your body, such as, my body is tired, my body is hungry, or my body is sore.

Fill in the blanks:
For example; I am: exhausted
I am: _____

I am: _____

I am: _____

Now remove the identification with your body:
My body is feeling: _____

My body is feeling: _____

My body is feeling: _____

How do you feel after doing this exercise? What insights occurred for you?

_____
_____

My form is perfect for me. I love this form. It is my ride in the river of space and time, in the river of life. I can love the sunset. I can love anything physical reality has to offer. I can love another. I can experience the drama of love and friendship. I feel distinct, in love with my experience of individuation.
    -A poem on the individuation of spirit in the body.

Repeat this meditation:
I am not the body; the body is mine.
    -Maharaj

Life is Leela

Leela in Sanskrit means *divine play*. It implies that life itself is not as we think it is. When we are Creator Beings life becomes a play, a dance, a game, a sport, an enjoyment – this is what it is meant to be. When we embody the Higher Self, and live the detachment that is innate in us, this truth becomes evident.

Believe it not, but once you have fully detached, your spirit, your embodied Higher Self, may occasionally enjoy the lived experience of something you once thought was an attachment. It may even guide you, provide a synchronicity, or even a miracle, all in the name of experiencing something you called an attachment, which it deemed to be fun.

We have to get to the place of detachment first but then your Consciousness might tell you to have an alcoholic drink to celebrate a success in life. It might enjoy that you go to coffee shops as a means of focusing on your creativity.

Your spirit manifested you into the physical for a reason, and that was to enjoy what it has to offer.

Try to not be dogmatic, or not to judge, or make assumptions about what can appear as an attachment. The point is, is the desire an intention of love. Having an alcoholic drink can be rooted in an intention of self-love to celebrate. While being attached is saying you always need an alcoholic drink to celebrate - see the difference.

Let your spirit be the one to tell you, not your mind. If you are one pointed towards God, Consciousness, your higher power, then what does this attachment look like? Are you still doing it? Or does it transform into a desire of Consciousness?

Now that we understand detachment it is time to experience our Source.

The Rising

There is a force in the Universe that supports you, that is there for you, that desires you to grow. This is your Higher Self, which is merged in the dimension of God, the unified field force; God/your Higher Self - the same thing. It is the limited human mind that tries to nitpick about which experience was God and which was the Higher Self, yet they are merged in the incomprehensible Unity being One and the same.

Your Higher Self is not the identity you know as yourself, but it is you. When you are not aware of its existence you project it outside of you as another force. When you can't embody the grandness of being God, either because you don't believe you are that, or you haven't yet experienced it, then the Higher Self becomes an outward experience of God. When you know exactly the power you are, that you are God, the mover of the physical world, then you embody the Higher Self, the portion of you that is the aware individuation of God. This is the play.

<u>You embody what you know you are, and what you can't believe you are you project outside of you.</u>

The qualities of God
Omnipotent – All Powerful
Omniscient – All Knowing
Omnipresent – Present Everywhere

As God-lets
Omnipotent – All Powerful - Visioning
Omniscient – All Knowing – Intuition (tuning into information in the unified field force through light and sound)
Omnipresent – Present Everywhere – Sight in no space and no time

When you can't embody these qualities, when you don't experience them as your own, then you project them as an outside force.

Ever had a streak of bad luck - a set of repeated synchronicities where the events of your life were not going your way. Maybe you believed God had it out for you, or "somebody," some spirit, was trying to tell you something. Your streak of bad luck very well could have been the manifestations of your own Higher Self that you were not listening to, which you then project outwards. In these moments we may not see how we are connected to, and are creating, the so-called streak of bad luck. It is in moments like these that I go within to understand what disconnected thoughts and feelings are creating these manifestations.

So, when you develop a relationship with God, and know God is there for you, loving you, you begin to embody the Higher Self.

The process of entrainment is when something with a weaker vibration begins to resonate with something that has a stronger vibration. We come to God as a method of entrainment to embody our Higher Selves.

Source is with you. Not for one moment will it ever leave you and be without you, even when you don't believe it, or feel you don't deserve it. Right from the moment you came to this Earth It has been with you and when you leave It leaves with you. This loving eternal embrace, eternal compassion, with care, and gentility, this is the Higher Self's embrace, this is God's embrace. Think, every moment, even when you think you don't deserve it, you are being loved.

Any idea that it is punitive, vindictive, or supports an us versus them mentality does not speak of a true experience of Source and is therefore made up in the mind of humankind.

You are the beloved, you are loved, you are the epitome of love, you are love personified, projected. The house of The Lord is you, your Consciousness. You are the Magus, you are the symbol of wisdom, you are the concentration of the Universe. You are infinite, and invincible, because you live in the house of The Lord. You cannot be anything short of that.
-Maharaj

Be aware that it's aware of you right now. Focus on your heart and say;

"I know unified field force, that you are aware of me. I know Higher Self, that you are aware of me. And I am aware of you."

Then feel within.

Yearning for Liberation

One day a wise sage was sitting on the banks of the Ganges. He was approached by a young man who was searching for God.
"Wise sage, can you tell me, does God exist?"
The sage, looking at the young man affectionately, asked, "How badly do you want to know?"
Thinking he was being played with, the young man chuckled and said, "I do want to know."
The sage replied, "Follow me," as he took the would-be student to the edge of the waters of the Ganges, and then began to walk in.
Perplexed, the young man walked in with him till they were both up to their chest in water.
Again, the sage asked, "How badly do you want to know that God exists?"
Chuckling again, he said "I want to know."
Unexpectedly, the sage dunked the young man's head in the water and held it there. He began to fight as he held his breath. Then, as the young man panged for air, and before he passed out, the sage pulled his head up and asked. "How badly did you want to breathe?"
Panting and flustered, he replied, "With all my life."
"That's how badly you need to want to find God."

You are breaking out of your ego, out of years of conditioning to create a paradigm shift, and that can't happen with mild interest or with ulterior motives.

Do you desire to break free from the illusion of physical reality to know your true Self? Write here, yes or no. _____

Do you desire to do so truthfully and authentically with no ulterior motive? Write here, yes or no. _____

If you said no to either of these then you won't be able to achieve your Rising. You can try the exercises but you won't get the full benefit of them. But I'll assume you said yes to both of these questions so we can move forward.

As long as you mean it to be true, say out loud;

> *I yearn to know what I am beyond the physical.*
> *I yearn to know my eternal Self.*
> *I desire to know what I am in between lives.*

Say out loud emphatically:
"I DESIRE TO BREAK FREE FROM THE ILLUSION OF PHYSICAL REALITY."

If you have any emotional pains, then you're caught in an illusion. Do you have any pains?

Do you believe you are limited and cannot change your circumstances? Then you are caught in an illusion.

You have long been lost in a hall of mirrors, lost in your own thought projections, and the only way out is to change which sense is guiding you, to create a paradigm shift, a reorientation of your sense of Self. You are your Being.

The Five Keys to Enlightenment

We have waited lifetimes for our evolution to culminate into our Rising. The information has always existed amongst us, the how-to, but we weren't ready to receive it. Here you're given the keys, but only you can open the door.

Your Rising is not in your mind. It is beyond the mind. These are the Five Keys to Enlightenment to open the door beyond your mind.

Let the riddle begin.

Key 1: Bhakti

Bhakti in Sanskrit means "devotion," or "worship." Worship simply means being "worthy of." You worship that which you love. When you love your spouse, you are worshiping them.

We bring close and begin to know that which we love. When we love someone or something, it becomes a part of our lives, and eventually it merges with our Being.

To bring us closer to our Source we look at our own personal description within. Each thought passes through the visual cortex of our brain so it can be helpful to reflect on what image we use for God.

An individual complained to Sri Ramakrishna that he found it impossible to turn his mind Godward. It was asked of him as to what was the thing or being that he loved most. The man pondered for a while and said that he was inordinately attached to a goat that he reared. A suggestion was then made to him to think of that goat as imbued with divinity and meditate on it. The man did so and had his mind slowly turned Godward.
    -Swami Chidbavanunda, commentary on the Bhagavad Gita

According to Dr. Andrew Newberg and Mark Waldman's book *How God Changes Your Brain,* Source has an incredible effect on the brain. One begins to formulate higher values that become real experiences in the brain by embodying them. For example, if Source to you is unlimited loving, then you awaken in you an idea of the experience of unlimited love. If Source is infinite to you then you awaken in you the experience of infinity. And likewise, if you believe Source judges you then you will judge yourself and others. See how that works.

Source is the highest ideal created in Self. As my teacher says, *The individual reaches the divinity he worships.* You bring That closer to you.

What is God to you?
What is Source to you?
What is the unified field force to you?

What image comes to mind? What feeling occurs for you?

Write down here an image you associate with God/Source/the unified field force. It can be vague if need be (a light, a cloud, a star), or it can be of a wise teacher, an image from nature, whatever suits you. Every thought has an image, which is yours for God? Take your time to contemplate this.

_____

_____

_____

What words do you use to describe your feeling of Source?

_____

_____

_____

_____

_____

You are loved and are a part of the whole.
You are loved because you are a part of the whole.

With your image and description of Source fill in the blanks. For example, if you said The Light describes your Source, then below write "The Light is the Creator."

_____ is the Creator. Contemplate on this. The Creator of everything surrounds you. But also, It is the Creator of your own world.

_____ is the preserver. It is the preserver of your world, the great maintainer.

_____ is the destroyer. It is the changer, creating the ending of one cycle and the beginning of the next. And It is also the changer of events and circumstances in your own world.

Describe in your own words what you think the above three statements mean.

_____

_____

_____

_____ is the Absolute (of time and space).

_____ is All knowledge.

_____ is the supreme level of Source Consciousness, beyond conceptualization.

_____ is the Indivisible Whole, which pervades the moving and nonmoving beings.

_____ is the Self within all beings.

_____ within is the God of the Universe.

_____ is beyond duality and is boundless and infinite.

_____, who are all the Mahavakyams.
Tat Tavm Asi: That thou Art, _____ is everything.
Ayam Atma Brahman, _____ is your Consciousness.
Aham Brahmasmi, _____ is You.

_____, who is One not Two, who is eternal, who is the witness of the intelligence of all beings and is beyond the states of the mind.

To end this exercise, choose a space, such as your altar you use for meditation, or if need be, you can use an empty wall. Do you have a physical image you can use, make, or purchase that represents your image of Source? If so, place it in front of you. If not, that is OK, just use your imagination.

Recite the above with your description of Source filled in. Then kneel on the ground, facing the wall, and slowly lower your forehead as you lay out your hands before you. Imagine your hands are touching your Source. Maybe it's the feet of your image, or it's hand, or if your image is abstract, such as light, imagine your hands are touching the light.

This is called *pranum* and is the ultimate action of surrender. You are multidimensional and the only way to awaken it is by surrender to it.

My nature is weighed down with the taint of feeblemindedness; my understanding is confused as to duty. I entreat you, say definitely what is good for me. I am your disciple. Do instruct me who has taken refuge in you.
-*Bhagavad Gita, 2.7*

The above line is the despondency of Arjuna to his Master Krishna. Arjuna is in crisis and surrenders to Krishna who is his Consciousness. This line is the feeling of surrender to your Source.

Without and within all Beings; the unmoving and also the moving, because of His subtlety He is incomprehensible; He is far and near.
   -Bhagavad Gita 13.15

   Consciousness is all there is;
      walking for Consciousness,
         thinking for Consciousness,
            eating for Consciousness,
               doing everything for Consciousness.
                  You become what you contemplate.

Key 2: Beyond Duality/Beyond Time -
One Who Is Free From the Pairs of Opposites and the Past, Present and Future

It is the direct cognition of the Atman which is always present in all thought. Everybody has some knowledge of this Ātman or Self, for, to deny the Self is to deny one's own existence. But at first its real nature is not known. Later on, when the mind becomes purer through Upasana and Tapas, the veil of ignorance is gradually withdrawn and the Self begins to reveal its real nature. A higher knowledge follows at an advanced stage, when the knowledge of the 'Self as mere witness' is seen as absorbing all other thoughts.

But the end is not yet reached. The idea of duality, such as 'I am the witness' ('I' and the 'witness'), is still persisting. It is only at the last stage when the knower and the known merge in the Self-effulgent Ātman, which alone ever is, and besides which nothing else exists, that the culmination is reached. This realization of the non-dual is the consummation of Aparokshânubhuti.
   -Commentary on the Aparokshanubhuti by Swami Vimuktananda

The world of the physical is bound by both duality (that is the opposing opposites; happy-sad, tall-short, male-female), and time (the past, present, and future). Yet, we originate first from the realm beyond, the Absolute, in which duality doesn't exist, and there is no time.

The past, present, and future in the Vedas are referred to as the three Guna's. When you have released yourself from them your mantra becomes the Word, you live in the Beingness of the I am.

It might be confusing to include the present in this understanding of time, because if time doesn't exist then isn't the present all we have? Even in the present, once you experience, you have an experiencer experiencing. Yet, whatever you are experiencing you are not that, it's not you. When we use Consciousness to think, our thoughts take form, reflecting either the duality and/or the past present or future. These thoughts are a limitation, and when there is a limitation there is an illusion.

Who is the I? The Higher Self is the I. The Unity is the I. When you experience that Consciousness, that is Samadhi; when you reveal your Self to yourself.

For this exercise, we seek a state of Consciousness before those thoughts bound by duality and time are made. To do so we will have to empty our cup, obviating everything we think we know.

My teacher would often retell this well-known ancient proverb;

Once, there was a wise Master that many people traveled to, seeking his help. One day a scholar came to the Master seeking advice.
"Teach me Master, the power of the ancients."
Soon it was obvious that the scholar was filled with his own opinions and knowledge. He constantly interrupted the Master with his own stories and failed to listen to his wisdom. The Master suggested they have tea. As the Master poured the tea, quickly it was full, yet he continued pouring, overflowing the cup, with its contents pouring on the table, on the clothes of the scholar, and onto the floor.
The scholar exclaimed, "What are you doing? Can't you see the cup is already full."
The Master said calmly and intently, "Yes, you are like this cup. So full of ideas that nothing can fill it. Come back to see me when your cup is empty."

Consciousness is beyond time, beyond the you formed from the past, or the anticipation of the future. We will need to empty our cup to experience something new, to break out of our existing paradigm, to experience a new truth. With your old ideas and concepts about yourself, it is impossible to do so.

This here is a 'beyond time - beyond duality' exercise;

Sit in your meditation posture. Close your eyes and focus on a few breaths. Now put aside any motive or intention in this exercise. Without having a cause, be still, alert, and fully aware. Now put aside your memory. Keep breathing in your belly. Now put aside your beliefs. Breathe in through your nose into your belly. And now put aside your ideology. Even, set aside your attachment to your memory, beliefs, and ideology being true. In this moment it's just you. Be still and aware. Even put aside those things which may be fact for you from personal experience. Just put them out of the way. They don't have to be untrue, just quite holding them as true. Release yourself from the attachment of wanting them to be true. Release yourself from any dominance of any idea of what was true for you.

Don't push to not have thoughts, don't try to experience anything. Just be. The realm of duality works in such a way that if you say 'peace,' then the potential for the opposite, 'chaos' automatically arises. Just remain in a non-questioning, observing state.

Regardless of your mind not being quiet, just pay full attention, remaining still and open. If you do this for a few seconds, something new will come through. Let whatever happens need to happen. It may be fleeting.

You may have touched something grander. I can't describe it for you. It is simply your I am. If you ever do this exercise with the intention to experience this, you won't be able to. You have to be intentionless.

Remain here in a non-questioning state, yet fully alert, and observing. Sit in the stillness. Don't force anything. Don't push, just exist, independent of anything or any ideas that once was. Now, you don't know anything. You are simply existing. It's here, where you know nothing that you can actually truly only know.

Here you are above the physical, above the dance of the pair of opposites, above duality. This is union.

Stay here as long as you desire. When you're ready, with your eyes still closed, focus on your breathing, and bring your hands to the ground as a way of slowly grounding you back into the physical world. After a breath open your eyes and come out.

Consciousness does not live in the past, the present, or the future. It does not understand time and space. It is. It was never born and it will never die. Consciousness is you and Consciousness is me. There was never a time that you were not and there will never be a time that you will cease to be. That is the feeling of Consciousness.
    -Tulshi Sen; Ancient Secrets of Success for Today's World

Because you add something to your "I," to your Aham, you receive blows from life. If you remain that pure "I," the pure I-consciousness, you are God. It is when you become a man or a woman, a swami or a professor, a doctor or an engineer that the pure "I" becomes the ego.
    -Swami Muktananda; I am That

The Story of the Walled City

There was a city surrounded by a wall so big that nobody could see what was outside the city. The citizens of the city could only see the sky and what was in the city. Everyone that scaled up the straight wall and stood on top of the wall, jumped off the wall. They never came back. So no one in the city knew what was on the other side of the wall. This got everybody curious and they wanted to find out what was there outside.

The Mayor of the City called a council meeting to find out ways and means to know what was outside the city. In the Council meeting a young man came up with a brilliant idea. He said, "If we select one of us to climb up the wall and before that person climbs the wall we should tie a rope to his feet, and when he jumps we will pull him back. This way we can find out what is there, outside the city."

Everybody clapped and gave him a standing ovation. The Council, owing to the young man's brilliance, selected him to do the job. They had their ceremony for this big occasion and they were waiting with controlled patience for all these rituals to be over with to find out what is out there.

The man scaled the wall. The whole population of the city watched with bated breath to know the truth. The man stood on top of the wall. The people below saw the man's face gleam with ecstasy. Like everyone before him, he too helplessly jumped. The city folks let out a grand cheer. He was pulled back and brought to the city square.

They asked, "Tell us, oh our Hero what did you see?"

The people waited for the Truth. The young man became silent. He could not say anything.

When you will know the Truth, you too will become silent.

There are no words in any language to express what you will experience, when you have scaled the wall of your mind through meditation and see what lies beyond. Anything you say will only sound like gibberish to those who don't know. Silence will prevail in your life and you will live in bliss.
    -Tulshi Sen; Ancient Secrets of Success for Today's World

You are not who you think you are. And your greatest joy is bringing who you really are into this world. We are a heart with a mind, not a mind with a heart.

Key 3: Identity

The Fourth Proclamation

You are God, the Source. The purpose of the fourth proclamation, dissolves your sense of separation and reveals your true identity that has always lived within. With this proclamation there is no difference between you and your Consciousness.

I introduce an ancient Sanskrit dictum as the fourth proclamation; **Aham Brahmasmi** (Source: Yajurveda, Brhadâranyaka Upanisad, 1.4.10).

Phonetically it is;

Ah-ham Brahm-ash-mee

Aham means I, and *Brahmashmi* means Am the Creator. Therefore, the meaning of this proclamation is I am the Creator.

When we realize our Consciousness is a part of the larger Consciousness, we become That. We are God.

Brahmavid Brahmaiva Bhavati - Knowledge of the Creator makes you the Creator

This proclamation imbues the meditator with the ultimate power of their identity as One with the Universe.

Repeat this Proclamation in your meditation by breathing in through your nose and on your exhale, say Aham Brahmashmi by elongating the vowels; not too slow and not too fast.

Just as the tree is to the leaf, or ocean to the wave of the ocean, or flame to the spark of the flame, we are God-lets, living out our existence within, as, and with Source, with all the same power to create our own Universe.

Your Consciousness is everywhere, and everywhen.

If you are God then how does God walk? How does God talk? How does God think? Contemplate on this.

Write here an issue you are currently facing in your life.
_____
_____

Write here how you think God, the power of the Universe within you, would handle it. What would the unified field, the Source, do or not do differently? Treat this exercise lightly, as there is no right answer. Its purpose is to get your mind thinking about this power you have within.

_____
_____
_____
_____
_____

All the power that ever was and will be is in you right now, it's just awaiting your recognition.

Look at the mountains, sky, stars, land and say I created that.
You are God. Look at the mountains, clouds, land, the stars and say I created that.
I created that.

Key 4: Pure Heart

Herein is expounded (the means of attaining to) Aparokshânubhuti (Self-realization) for the acquisition of final liberation. Only the pure in heart should constantly and with all effort meditate upon the truth herein taught.
  - *Aparokshânubhuti; Verse 2*

Inside your heart cave you are innocent, regardless of what you think you've done to any other while acting without the knowledge of who and what you are.

Inside your heart cave you are a child that loves to play.

Inside your heart cave you care about the well-being of others.

Inside you are pure, a child at best, confident as a part of the Universe.

Reflect on the feeling of innocence.

Write here whatever images or associations come to mind when you reflect on the feeling of innocence.

_____
_____
_____

Within Bhakti is love, love for everything and everyone. This is the pure in heart.

To open ourselves to our inner, innocent, child-self try this exercise.

Describe something you have done or do that you would relate as being child-like fun?

_____
_____
_____

If you can't think of anything, what would it look like to do something that has child-like fun?

_____
_____
_____

In the joyful love of freedom, the child wants to play. Describe something you have done or do that provides you with a sense of child-like freedom?

_____
_____
_____

If you can't think of anything, what would it look like to do something that provides you with a sense of child-like freedom?

_____
_____
_____

Have you ever felt like you have been cared for by the Universe, by God? Did an event or series of events align just right to make you feel that something was watching over you? What did that feel like?

_____
_____
_____

If not, could you imagine this experience? What would it feel like if it did occur to you?

Describe a time when you were filled with joy.

If you can't think of a time, what would it look like to be filled with joy?

According to the teachings of the Toltecs, the feeling of quiet and deep joy means that one has an abundance of pure spiritual light in one's spiritual heart. It is the evidence that one has chosen the path of the heart and is doing everything right, moving along the path of their destiny.

Do you feel deep joy in your heart? If yes, what is it you're doing right?

If not, what do you feel you need to change to feel that deep joy, that deep spiritual light?

Think of your mind as something that needs to be protected. What you focus on or put your mind towards will colour it. So, not to create any kind of judgment or resistance, but try to avoid entertainment or videos of violence or disturbing content. Seeing these images can leave imprints in the mind that affect our emotional well-being. Also, to have a pure heart we need to leave our hurts and angers behind us, or any idea that we are struggling in the world. This is the importance of the previous chapter *Ocean of the Mind*, and the next chapter on Visioning because a pure heart does not have a fight inside. Learning to leave these behind will make space in your mind to hold the pure heart.

Key 5: There is No I

My Self is the Self in all Beings.

Repeat *My Self is the Self in all Beings*.

Right before you interact with someone or a group of people in public, bringing to mind your experience meditating on Aham Brahmasmi, and your experience meditating beyond time and duality, say to yourself as you approach them; *My Self is the Self in all Beings*.

How does it feel to do this?

_____

_____

_____

With the realization of God everything undergoes transformation for the Jnani. It is God Himself that has become the phenomenal Universe and all the beings in it. The son is then perceived as the boy Krishna. Father and Mother undergo metamorphosis as the Divinity. The wife is no more his mate; he sees the Cosmic Mother in her. Recognizing God in all, adoration to Him takes place through the worshipful service of all.
    -Sri Ramakrishna, commentary on the Bhagavad Gita

But when he…thinks 'I alone am this world! I am all!' — that is his highest world. Now, this is the aspect of his that is beyond what appears to be good, freed from what is bad, and without fear…Here a father is not a father, a mother is not a mother, worlds are not worlds, gods are not gods, and Vedas are not Vedas. Here a thief is not a thief, a murderer is not a murderer, an outsider is not an outsider, a pariah is not a pariah, a recluse is not a recluse, and an ascetic is not an ascetic. Neither the good nor the bad follows him, for he has now passed beyond all sorrows of the heart. So did Yajnavalkya instruct him; "This is his highest goal! This is his highest attainment! This is his highest world! This is his highest bliss!
    -Brihadaranyaka Upanishad, 4.3.20-32

    Your individuality is preventing you from full recognition of your Godhood. I am the Creator, Aham Brahmasmi, is the default mantra; this is the ceasing of existence, this is immense love. When you have engaged in immense love, then there is no You and no I. That is the goal is to loose the identity. This is Samadhi.

Summary of the 5 Keys of Enlightenment

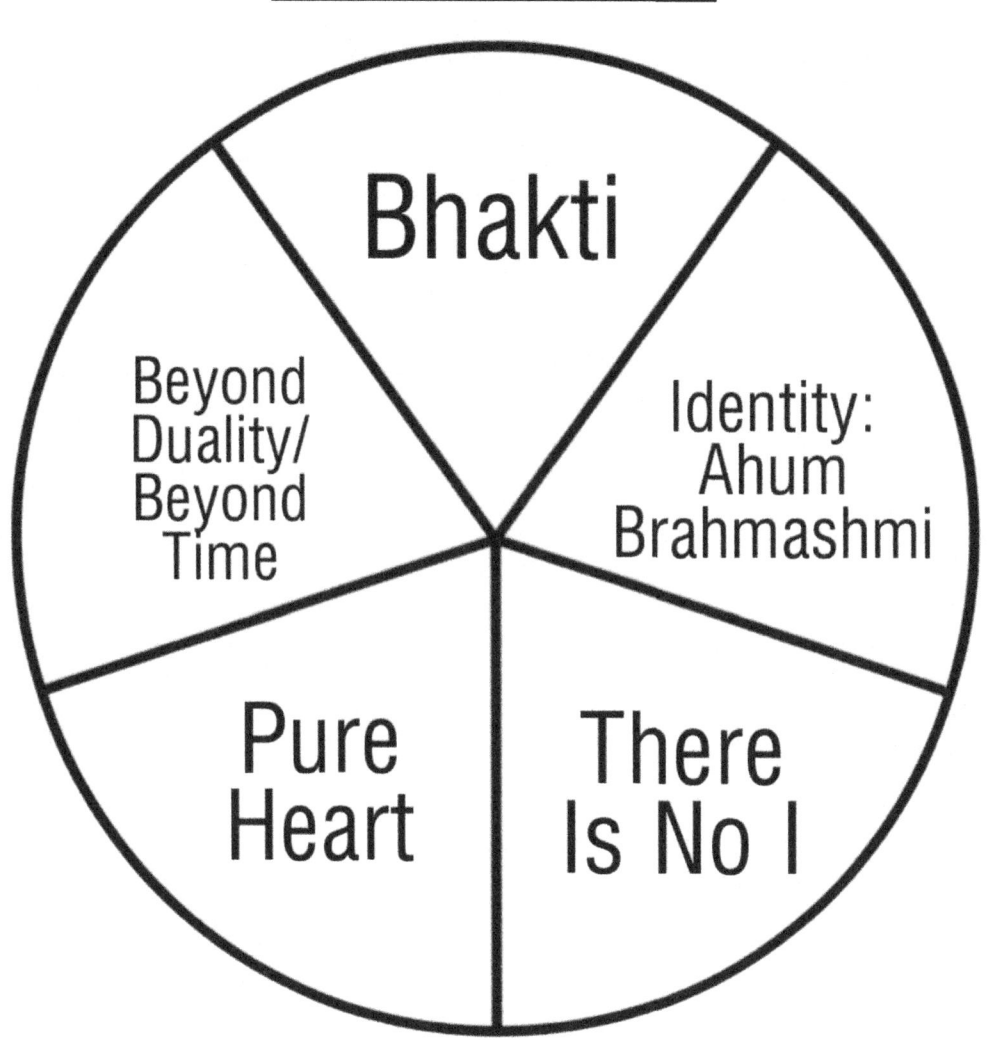

- Bhakti
- Identity: Ahum Brahmashmi
- There Is No I
- Pure Heart
- Beyond Duality/ Beyond Time

The 5 Keys of Enlightenment are not something you will master over a weekend, but that will deepen over your lifetime. The more they are practiced the greater you will experience your connection to the living Universe. As life circumstances change and the events in our world challenge us, we always have these keys that hold our power to guide us. These are the tenets you will always come back to, as you exercise your divinity in life, either through this book or others.

The Dimensions of the Universe Exist in the Incomprehensible Unity of Love

All experiences are Source. You are Source and everything you do is Source doing it for Source. Your actions are its actions; *I do nothing of myself, the Source that dwells in me does all the Work.*

The aware Universe is experiencing itself through you, uniquely from your perspective, and all humans are Source uniquely experiencing from their perspective, and the Unity we form together is also uniquely expressing and experiencing Source.

You are an integral part of the whole. That makes you important. You play a role like a cog in a clock. Without it there is a gap and the machine doesn't work.

The spark of the fire can light another fire, yet it does not diminish the fire that it came from. This is Universal Love. In Unity nothing diminishes, nothing is lessened. Only in Unity can you have an unlimited numbers of variations of a thing, and at the same time all those individual variations make up a whole.

You are One with the head Source, God the living Universe. We are also One with the Head Source, God, the living Universe. You and us come from the same source. We are all One, part of the One. That makes you our brothers and our friends. | The experience of Godhead is one that is reciprocal. When we live for the advancement and evolution of God, we live for the advancement and evolution of ourselves. When we live for the advancement and evolution of ourselves we live for the advancement and evolution of God. It is a shared Unity of experience. This and That, That and This simultaneously. | Right now you are in Unity. You live in a shared Unity Universe. Your experiences are Gods experiences.

-The Mystic Book

As beings that are living "cells" of the Conscious Universe, we are all splendid, remarkable, and magnificent. ALL our actions are simply learned experiences that don't affect Consciousness, which lives in a completed state in the Absolute. We are loved because we are a part of the All by the All, with no fault seen in anything we could label so, because the purpose of life is the joy of manifesting and experiencing in the relative, beyond ideas of morality. Meaning even the worst human you can think of is unconditionally loved by the Conscious Universe. And this is because in the physical realm we use that "negative" behaviour of the other to determine who we choose to Be. We choose how to act in the physical realm in response to their behaviour, therefore they help us define ourselves. This is the case for all your relationships, that their joy is in the defining of Self. Our joy is taking the unlimited Universe, and using it to create ourselves, to define our Self. In a way not comprehensible to your mind, you love the person who is giving the behaviour you deem to be negative because they help you and humanity define who we want to Be.

Can you think of the "worst person" who you would describe as having negatively affected your life? Right now, take a second and think about that person who you would define this way.

And then ponder that your Higher Self loves them for the role they play in helping you grow. This is the God level. From this perspective it is obvious that all of life is just a play.

This may be hard to imagine, but if we can't experience the love of the Universe as unconditional then we project the only experience of love we know, which came from our parents, and then we treat God the same, thinking It's love roots in conditions of judgment, expectations, and assumptions. Yet, this does not speak of a conscious aware Universe with which we are all apart.

It is incomprehensible that Source will judge, and It has no cause to punish. Without accepting this in some way fear will dominate our experience of love. This is the importance of meditation on Unity, as the unconditional love of the Universe lives here.

Recall your experience, meditating on Tat Tavm Asi, that thou art, Consciousness is everything. Now with Aham Brahmasmi that Unity, that intelligent love is you. That truth and power is You. It is love in Unity, like the tree loves the leaf - and it is available.

We can trust Source. This means that we can trust that everything that happens to us is for our own highest good. An inherent fear exists within us if we cannot feel that we are loved and that we can trust.

Describe an issue you face right now.

_____

_____

Can you see how your Higher Self brought you this issue? That it is there for your own highest good? Ponder and describe here how you think that could be. What is it that you gain from your issue? Maybe it's a strength of character, or a resilience. Whatever comes to mind, write it here.

_____

_____

If you couldn't answer the above question, no problem, that is the mystery of life. And if you found this hard, that is OK. Just ponder over time how this challenge could be there for your own highest good. That eventually it guides you in some way towards the embodiment of your own Higher Self.

A deep-seated fear can leave us if we can believe in the Unconditional Love of the Universe, and trust in the events that happen to us, that they are there to guide us towards the embodiment of our Higher Self. Do you trust life?

It starts by recognizing your own Higher Self loves those people and experiences that gave you reason not to trust. This is the play.

Trust the Universe, believe in the Love of the Universe, and believe it is Unconditional.

The shepherd will never leave his sheep…The metaphor of the sheep and the shepherd continues even to this moment and unto all eternity…The shepherd will risk his life and will not rest till he collects the last of his sheep. He will carry his sheep on his shoulder.
   -Maharaj

Loving Unconditionally

If love has conditions, then it is not love it is a transaction, and a transaction is not love.
   -Maharaj

My Master has a great story, about the Jar of Marmalade;

"A long time ago I use to know an elderly lady. I would say she would be very close to 90 years of age. One day when I went to visit her she told me "Last night I couldn't fulfill my passion!" I kept silent. And she went on and said "You see an hour before I go to bed I like to have toast with marmalade on it. I got a new jar of marmalade. I couldn't open the jar; it was shut too tight. So, I only had dry toast then I went to sleep." That was her passion. "I feel too weak" she said, "to unscrew the lid of the jar". So, I asked her "show me the jar". I opened the jar for her. And then I spent some time with her reading a part of her book for the seventh time, Charles Dickens Tale of Two Cities, and a particular part she wanted me to read the beginning and the end."

"And then after that, as I was walking down the street, it struck me. I realized, what is the problem with me? I felt like the jar of marmalade. The marmalade is the metaphor for love. It is the sole purpose of the jar to contain the marmalade and dispense the marmalade and I realized that we are containers of love and our only purpose of life is to love and pour out love. Our jar has been tight shut by time and our past conditioning. And we cannot open up to be loved and love, then we are afraid to love because we feel that if we try too hard, we will break the jar. That's us. As the lady told me at that time "I was afraid to use too much force, I might break the jar.""

"We end up living a life not fulfilling our purpose and we look for purpose everywhere else. Because our jar has been shut too tight. We stay on the shelf and instead seek love. <u>We have to be love. Then we shall serve our purpose to become the Beloved.</u>"

"So, the next day I went back to the elderly lady and gave her a jar opener. I decided to open up my jar. I found that I have to distribute jar openers throughout the world. That is my purpose."

   I am going to repeat this line of my Guru's. Love is our purpose. So because we choose not to love, we look for purpose everywhere else. We stay on the shelf and instead seek love, but we have to be love. Then we shall serve our purpose to be the God within us.

Can you relate to this line? That's OK, as many of us can. Be honest with yourself and describe something in which you seek love for in your life.

_____

_____

Now, take a moment to imagine that thing with which you seek love for, you changed to instead Being love. Write here what it looks like to change to Being love for that which you once sought love.

_____

_____

Did you notice any changes or sensations in your body from this imagination?

_____

_____

As long as you have the feeling of duality, the feeling that one human being is different from another, that one class is different from another, you cannot experience real happiness. The sense of otherness is the source of all fear, of all suffering, and of all sin. However, as you practice Hamsa, the consciousness of equality dawns in a natural manner.
    -Swami Muktananda; I am That

    Everyone around you is an energy form, a spirit, and not the body, in Unity with their environment, even if they don't know it. That Unity is an aspect of nature – everyone is an aspect of nature, and in Unity with it. When you see this, you understand we are all family, you feel it innately, without thought.

    How similar we all are; we all dream at night, have aspirations, and hold close the people we care about. Life is all about focus, and if we focus on why we are separate, we create separation. If we focus on why we are the same then we bring ourselves together and experience Unity. To live from unconditional love, we are always looking for our similarities, not differences.

    When you judge another know it is a part of yourself that you judge. Someone might do something that you might call stupid, such as cut you off while driving, or leave plates on a table, try not to form judgements. If it puts you out a little and not a lot, try not to form thoughts about it. If it puts you out a lot, say something, in a manner that doesn't condescend.

    If we are all one then we are each teaching each other something. What is it that your being taught?

Loving the Collective

Put yourself in a place of human gathering, maybe at a coffee shop, or a market, or a restaurant and feel the love, if you can, that seeps through all the friendships and connections. There is so much to be grateful for in this environment. See someone who is happy, see the friendships and families being enriched, even though they are people you have never met or talked to. Be grateful for the peace.

As you look around, ask yourself, *what can I give these people?* You don't have to create an answer, nor act on it if you do. The point is to simply create an intention within, to challenge our brain's tendency, made from years of unconscious conditioning, that privately thinks about what it can get out of our relationships and interactions with others.

Continuing to look around say *My Self is the Self in all Beings.* Can you see the Self in you is the Self in everyone around you?

Do this exercise again, looking at the people around you, but now say;

> *My Self is the Self in all Beings.*
> *What can I give these people?*

This time allow for an intention of giving to expand. It could be to give anything; kindness, helpfulness, something to uplift. Again, you don't have to act on it, just allow the intention to be created.

How does it feel to do this exercise?

This here is a meditation to expand our love for the collective;

Sit in your meditation posture. Close your eyes and spend a moment focusing on your breath. Begin by meditating on Tat Tavm Asi, either out loud or quietly. Focus on the feeling of Unity. Try not to move forward until you've caught a glimpse of Unity.

Now think of someone whom you love besides your partner. See this person in your mind's eye. Ponder that this person is a spirit in a body, an energy form in Unity, even if they don't know it. They are family. Then say, "I see the Self in me is the Self in you." Then in your imagination give them something. It can be anything imaginable. It could be love, or kindness, or gratefulness as a ball of light passed on to them, or it could be a practical gift that helps or uplifts them in their world.

Now bring this love to someone neutral. This person may have been the barista who got you your coffee, or the movie ticket assistant, or the grocery store clerk. Someone whom you don't have negative or positive feelings for. Visualize this person and ponder that they are a spirit in a body, an energy form in Unity, even if they don't know it. They are family. Then say, "I see the Self in me is the Self in you." Then in your imagination give them something. It can be anything imaginable. It could be love, or kindness, or gratefulness as a ball of light passed on to them, or it could be a practical gift that helps or uplifts them in their world.

Now bring this love to someone difficult, someone who irritates you or annoys you. This may be tricky. It is most helpful to think of someone whom you have a difficult relationship with in which you would like to make better. Visualize this person and ponder that they are a spirit in a body, an energy form in Unity, even if they don't know it. They are family. Then say, "I see the Self in me is the Self in you." Then in your imagination give them something. It can be anything imaginable. It could be love, or kindness, or gratefulness as a ball of light passed on to them, or it could be a practical gift that helps or uplifts them in their world. Be aware of what emotions arise for you. You are simply seeing their truth, and not condoning behaviour that has hurt you.

Now begin to visualize yourself levitating, rising upwards. If you are in a room with people, see them. If not, go to the height in which you see the building you're in, or the neighborhood you're in if you're in a house. See whatever group of people that are in your local vicinity. Visualize these people and ponder that they are all spirits in bodies, energy forms in Unity, even if they don't know it. They are family. Then say, "I see the Self in me is the Self in you." Then in your imagination give them all something. It can be anything imaginable. It could be love, or kindness, or gratefulness as a ball of light passed on to each of them in a single instant, or it could be a practical gift that helps or uplifts all of them in their world. We are all living beings, all wanting to love and be loved, all seeking happiness in our own way.

Now rise even further to a height in which you can see the town or city you are in. Visualize your community and ponder that they are all spirits in bodies, energy forms in Unity, even if they don't know it. They are family. Then say, "I see the Self in me is the Self in all of you." Then in your imagination give them all something. It can be anything imaginable. It could be love, or kindness, or gratefulness as a ball of light passed on to each of them in a single instant, or it could be a practical gift that helps or uplifts all of them in their world.

Now rise even further until you have a full view of the land or country you are in. Maybe you are now on the edge of space, or in space. Visualize the land and all the people in it and ponder that they are all spirits in bodies, energy forms in Unity, even if they don't know it. They are family. Then say, "I see the Self in me is the Self in all of you." Then in your imagination give them all something. It can be anything imaginable. It could be love, or kindness, or gratefulness as a ball of light passed on to each of them in a single instant, or it could be a practical gift that helps or uplifts all of them in their world.

Lastly, rise far enough out into space to see the planet Earth below you. Think about all the different human beings, all the friends and families. Visualize all the people on the planet and ponder that they are all spirits in bodies, energy forms in Unity, even if they don't know it. They are family. Then say, "I see the Self in me is the Self in all of you." Then in your imagination give them all something. It can be anything imaginable. It could be love, or kindness, or gratefulness as a ball of light passed on to each of them in a single instant, or it could be a practical gift that helps or uplifts all of them in their world.

Float back down over the land or county you're in. Say, "We are all family. I see the Self in me is the Self in all of you."

Now float back down over your community. Say, "We are all family. I see the Self in me is the Self in all of you."

Float further down over your building or neighborhood, seeing those in your vicinity. Say, "We are all family. I see the Self in me is the Self in all of you."

Now bring yourself down, and into the room you are in. While here, take a deep breath. Now, ponder that everyone you have ever interacted with and will continue to interact with is a spirit in a body, an energy form in Unity. They have always been and always will be a part of the family.

Take a few moments to sit with this experience. And when you're ready, come out of the meditation.

Write here what this experience was like for you.

Below is the *Prayer for Peace,* which due to its anonymous writer, was once mistakenly attributed as the *Prayer of St. Francis*. Though that shouldn't stop us from being inspired by it, as it is an empowering poem that speaks of selfless love. The writer of this poem sees other as the Self. Read each line slowly and contemplate on its meaning.

The Prayer for Peace

Lord make me an instrument of Thy Peace
Where there is hatred, let me sow Love;
Where there is injury, pardon;
Where there is doubt, faith;
Where there is despair, hope;
Where there is darkness, light;
Where there is sadness, joy
O Divine Master,
Grant that I may Not so much seek to be consoled as to console;
To be understood as to understand;
To be loved as to love.
For it is in giving that we receive,
It is in pardoning that we are pardoned,
And it is in dying to Self that we are born to eternal life.

Communicating with Source

You may ask, if Source is everything and it is aware of me then why don't I experience a direct communication, such as a manifestation of itself showing me it is aware and proving its existence?

You need to experience yourself as Source, and you can only do that by experiencing it internally. The moment you witness a miracle externally, say someone demonstrating they are God, you immediately create an idea about it, and then you have just limited the unlimited within.

Source will never materialize in a way to prove itself to us, as it would defeat the purpose of learning how to experience Source's presence on the inside. I have experienced physics defying miracles, but they never occurred because the Universe was trying to prove something to me; I believed and then the Universe showed itself. The Universe simply and only responds to how you think of it. If you believe the world around you is alive then it begins to act like it, in relationship to you.

Asking Questions and Getting Guidance

The Universe is always listening to you and giving you what you want, or it could be said you are always giving yourself what you want. All of life is a communication with the conscious Universe, with the Source.

What did the Universe say to you today?

The Universe communicates to us through feeling, through our Being state, and through pictures in our imagination. This is our Consciousness, which is One with the Universe. The Universe also communicates to us through the events of our lives, and through the people with which we interact with.

In the Absolute, the Source of your Consciousness, the outcomes of all personal problems and issues are known as they have already resolved themselves. Therefore, we rely on our feelings, feel what we are Being, or seek an image from our subconscious, to peer into the possible outcomes and to choose best.

If you're facing a dilemma, rely on your feeling, or feel what you are Being - this is the Universe communicating to you. Your best friend is the Universe, because you are That.

If you are scared, rely on your feeling, not your mind or your emotions. The Universe is alive and communicates through feeling. If you need to, ask for protection.

If you have been hurt and the emotional pain is hard to bear, rely on the Universe. Feel your feelings in those times. Emotional pain is as real as we want it to be, or as we need it to be. And there is also a Universe to rely on; a friend in times of need.

If you're put on the spot, call upon your Source by seeing its image or invoke its feeling. When you rely, how do you feel like responding to your call on the spot?

Have a difficult question, something frivolous, even something detailed about your work? Ask it to Source, ask the Universe, see what the answer is.

You could also try writing to the Universe. Either before you go to bed or before your meditation, in a journal or on a pad of paper, write down a question. Above the question, title it *Question for the Conscious Universe* or whatever you feel addresses your Source, as a means to set an intention. Connect with Unity and be as specific as you can in your question.

Be open also to a message from the Conscious Universe in answer to your question. Have an expectation that an answer will be received, and be open to synchronicities, unexpected feelings, or a message to emerge from your subconscious.

You could also ask Source to provide you with an answer to your issues in a meditation. Ask the question to the center of your heart, your Being.

You can also go a step further and receive writing from the Universe. Again, in a journal or on a pad of paper, write at the top of the page a title such as *Question for the Conscious Universe*, or whatever you feel addresses your Source. Then write down a question below. Connect with Unity when asking the question. Then write down the first thing that comes to you without thinking. Even if you felt nothing has come to you, just write. If you feel you're thinking about it, put the pen down. At first you may only get small pieces of information, but as you get better at the practice of putting aside your thinking those glimpses will become larger.

In all these ways the Universe can assist you.

The Messages in Synchronicities

A synchronicity will have exactness of timing and obviousness of meaning, with a precision more unlikely than the most improbable event.

I use an approach of loosely applying a 1 in 5 statistical significance to determine if a synchronicity is a meaningful event. If a chance of a synchronicity occurring in that exact moment in space and time is less than 1 in 5, then it is statistically significant, meaning the Universe converged to express a personal meaning making event.

For example, one night you dream that your grandma has died. Then in the morning you get a phone call that your grandma has unexpectedly passed away. Having never dreamt of this before, and not expecting her to pass away at that time, then it is a chance below 1 and is statistically significant.

Obviously, I wouldn't conduct an actual statistical study of the synchronicity, but I would use a best guess from logical deduction of what I know of the probabilities for any said events to converge exactly at that moment in space and time.

Another example, you ask the Universe for guidance on a career choice, then out of the blue you talk with a random stranger at a coffee shop who turned out to be in the line of career you were considering. You have never asked for career guidance from the Universe before, you rarely talk with strangers at coffee shops, and you didn't expect to learn of one's career, then it is a chance below 1 and is statistically significant.

If a synchronicity had a chance of less than one and five, of occurring right in that moment, right at that time, right in that place, in response to something very direct and personal to your own meaning making world, then it is statistically significant. And it could have been in response to a thought, desire, Being state, or a question you had.

The next step is the most important;

ACCEPT IT 100% AS A COMMUNICATION.

From what, is another matter; it could be your own Higher Self, from Source, or even an invisible entity, such as a guide, as any of these have the ability to use synchronicities as a means to either fulfill your desires or thoughts, or as a method of communication or both.

What if you know it was a synchronicity but are unclear on what its message is?

Regardless of the cause of a meaning making synchronicity in space and time, it is always a manifestation of you and your relationship with the Universe. Think of them as symbolic, as if they occurred in a dream. Then what does it symbolically say to you? What in your thought and feeling is it in response to? The answer to knowing the purpose of a synchronicity is often in the very thoughts and feelings that occurred for you in the moment of its manifestation. If you experienced a synchronicity, take a second to reflect on your feelings in the moment. What was your first thought you had as soon as the synchronicity occurred?

As Creator Being's, when we rely on our Source we have the potential to create a magical flow in our lives. As my Guru says, *Miracles should be a common occurrence*. When you live as a Creator Being, synchronicities are an everyday part of your existence.

Limitless Love is Not Martyrdom

A common misconception is that to love others unconditionally is to allow others to do what they want at the expense of our own feelings. That it's OK if you get hurt as long as you showed the other unconditional love. Unconditional love is not martyrdom. No one should sacrifice their emotions, as all that gets created is resentment, and then you have not loved but hurt the other by hurting yourself. Unconditional love is about loving yourself and the other as yourself. People can hurt you and they should be told not to hurt you. The same way your internal dialogue can hurt you, and you need to learn to stop or change the dialogue.

Here is a great story about a snake, told by my Master, which captures the confusion between unconditional love and martyrdom.

This story is of a great sage of India. There was a small village, the village had lots of children but these children couldn't come out to play in the field because there's a snake out there, bit everybody that came. One day a sage was passing through the village, he didn't see children playing. He didn't hear laughter. So, he asked the village people, "What happened? Is there any children in this place?" They said, "Yes, but there is a big snake out there who comes and bites them." "Where does he live." "He lives in that big hole behind that big hill." He called. The snake came out and bowed to him. He said, "Master, what can I do for you?" He said, "You've been bad. You have been biting all these children, the children can't come out to play." He said, "That's my nature." "I bless you, don't bite." "I take your blessings, I won't bite."

On his return journey he saw the children playing. "Where's the snake?" he asked the children "Oh, he must be in his hole." And asked the snake, "Come out." The snake came out. He was all injured, bleeding, skin got ruptured in many places, his head was bruised. He said, "What happened to you?"

The snake said, "Master it's all your fault. You told me not to bite. So, I went out to play with the children, and the children threw stones and kicked me, and I wouldn't bite them back."

"But I never told you not to hiss. You can hiss but don't bite." And he left.

He would continue;

You don't need to attack people. You have been given a hiss to defend yourself from unwarranted attack. Be stern, don't be a martyr. Don't say beat me up I'm good, I am nonviolent. Don't threaten, hiss.

You are More Than You Know

Knowing our magnitude is our salvation. We truly are magnificent Beings, much larger than we believe ourselves to be, with impeccable joy in our grandness. This is the joy in celebrating true Source Consciousness, the joy of our grandness. It may be hard to hear how grand you are, especially if you think you've done some not so grand things. In time you will be able to hold your experiences that have caused you pain, and maybe pain to others, within the same experiences that cause you joy and love. Life is a play, and the play is the joy. Without our labels or judgments about our experiences we can see just how grand the experience of life truly is.

As my teacher says, *Happiness is the joy of being more than you are.* That is the joy of being yourself; embracing being more than you experience you are. He would end this statement with, *There is no need to struggle.*

To live in the experience of unconditional Universal love one must come to terms with their own grandness; that we are important in even our smallest way to the Universe, and that we are multidimensional Beings, already existing in our perfect state that we are not aware of. This is a truth and not a fantasy. Your perfection is here and it is you. The key is to know the qualities of you that are God Self-expressed, and that there is a perfect space in the Absolute where you are these things always.

As written in *Conversations with God (1996)*;

You are goodness and mercy and compassion and understanding. You are peace and joy and light. You are forgiveness and patience, strength and courage, a helper in time of need, a comforter in time of sorrow, a healer in time of injury, a teacher in times of confusion. You are the deepest wisdom and the highest truth; the greatest peace and the grandest love. You are these things. And in moments of your life you have known yourself as these things.

We Are Creator Beings With the Power to Create Reality Through Visioning

You can have anything you desire.
You can live with your heart fulfilled.

It's simple; feel, Be, and imagine the future event as if it's the present, then know it to be true. Rely on the Higher Self, God, the Universe, whatever it is for you, that experiences your Vision with you.
This relationship creates an assurity.

It's simple yet challenging for our minds to understand because it is grounded within time, while our Consciousness is not.
Yet, the rewards are mastery over our life.

There is a grand desire in the Universe for you to be fully released from any inhibitions and know with security that anything you desire can be created. This is the role of Visioning.

So, let's get into it
…

How to Vision

Below is a breakdown of Visioning into five components. These exercises themselves are not Visioning but are to get you familiar with its different skill sets, so when you combine them, they will facilitate your success.

1) You Are Surrounded by the Unreal

Success in Visioning begins with accepting that the world around us is an illusion. In the first chapter we explored the simulation hypothesis, which leads us to the knowledge that creation is happening now - right now. Matter is created out of an energy of potentialities. The Universe is Consciousness which is the same energy as you, and is more receptive to feelings and thoughts than we can imagine. The imagination on the inside is more real than the world around you on the outside.
In that first chapter was a simple exercise which might be helpful to briefly review;

Take a moment to look at the world around you, the tables and chairs, or whatever you're looking at, and understand that every single point, every atom, and every little piece of everything, is instantly connected to the thing that's generating it, that's creating it. The Source is there right now, around you.

Knowing that the creation of the Universe is happening all around us in the present moment, and that imagination is more real than matter, we can then live in a place where we create all things around us, even though we are surrounded by the illusion of the static physical world.

2) **The Being State**

Understanding our Being state is essential for Visioning. I recommend reviewing the Being State section and exercises in the second chapter.

3) **Imagination**

Putting effort into specific and detailed imagination is crucial for successful Visioning. Below is a fun visualization to help expand your imaginative potential.

Close your eyes and breathe through your nose and into your diaphragm, slowly in and out. There is no right or wrong way to imagine, don't be hard on yourself, and try not to judge or criticize yourself. If there is something you cannot see or visualize just take note and try your best.

Imagine a triangle. See a red triangle. When seeing this triangle see it any way you can. If you can see it in your mind's eye that's great, yet if you cannot, try to imagine seeing it on a movie or tv screen. See this triangle any way you can. See its shape, see its colour. What is it made of? Let your answer be whatever comes to mind. Now let go of the image of the triangle. Now see a white circle form in your mind's eye or on your mental screen. Again, observe this image and see it fully, any circle will do. See the white of this circle. What is it made of? Now let go of the circle. This time see a blue cube, any shade of blue, see the cube. Now see it rotating, just rotating in empty space. Now let go of this image.

Now imagine it is wintertime and you are out in the countryside on a snowy field; see the grey sky. Feel the crisp cold air. See your breath exhale. Walk forward, feeling the snow below you. Feel the snow crunch beneath your boots. Somewhere there is a radio playing, "Jingle Bells." Hear what it sounds like. Now let that image fade away.

Now you are on a warm tropical beach. Feel the warmth of the sun on your skin. See the blue sky and bright sun. See the ocean waves rolling onto the shore, one right after another. Stand here and watch the waves, feel the warm sand beneath your feet. Now let this image fade away.

Now in the empty space in front of you hear a dog barking. Now smell smoke. Now taste a candy cane. Now hear a car horn. Now let go.

Come out of this meditation when you are ready.

Write here what that was like for you.

_____
_____
_____

There are abundant brain studies and much medical research that demonstrate when we imagine a scenario our brain and body responds as if it is real, and this is the same for when we Vision. Take a moment to try this exercise;

Close your eyes, breath into your diaphragm, and take a moment to observe any sensations in your body. Now Vision the end of your day. See yourself home at night. Maybe you are with your partner or maybe alone, just witness whatever routine is a part of your nighttime activities. See this future moment, but imagine it is right now. Fully immerse yourself. Give yourself a moment to experience this. Now take note of how your body feels, of any changes that may have occurred from when you first observed your body. Now open your eyes.

What changes do you notice in your body when you do this exercise?

_____
_____
_____

  Visioning is a projection of the future yet as if it is the present. But the image you project about the future as the present, is the present for your Consciousness, and this is because it has access to all time. The Universe, connected to your Consciousness, snaps your desired future projection into place via synchronicity, through the illusion of linear time. In the first chapter, in the section titled *We are Multidimensional Beings*, my Guru relays an exercise to experience the timelessness of our imagination. It would be helpful to review that exercise now to understand that the Vision is created in the timelessness of imagination.

It is important to understand that when you are Visioning the future event, seeing the detail in your imagination, and feeling it as if it is the present, you're actually creating that future event, which is not the future at all but the present, because there is no time, even though your senses haven't experienced it yet.

4) Source Is Aware of Your Desire

Like a film projector from our heart, the Universe mirrors the Being and images it receives from us and turns it into our reality. Your world becomes a reflection of your Being. Your outward life is a reflection of your internal life. It is the time between linear cause and effect that makes it difficult to see this relationship.

A circumstance does not make a person, it reveals them to themselves.
 - *James Allen*

We are the creator of the events of our lives. I know it can be hard to hear this, especially when there are circumstances we have endured that make us feel like we did not create them. And we may be boggled by how we created our circumstances when others are involved in its manifestation. The answer is that you and everyone you know are One with the Universe, meaning literally, we are Him/Her/It/That. Being the creators of the events of our lives is both the greatest power that we can have and the grandest form of responsibility.

If this is your first-time hearing this then it may be hard to believe. Therefore, it might be easier to accept when you look at your own past and try and see how it might have been possible that you created the events that happened to you. Can you remember a time when you desired something and it came to be, very similar or exactly as you imagined it. At the time that it occurred did you think that you created it? Did it feel that way for you?

Below list three negative events that have recently happened to you and see if you can remember any thoughts you had before the event occurred.

Negative Event:
_____
_____
_____

What thoughts did you have before the event occurred?
_____
_____
_____

Negative Event:
_____
_____
_____

What thoughts did you have before the event occurred?

Negative Event:

What thoughts did you have before the event occurred?

Do the same with three positive events that you have had recently.

Positive Event:

What thoughts did you have before the event occurred?

Positive Event:

What thoughts did you have before the event occurred?

_____

_____

Positive Event:

_____

_____

What thoughts did you have before the event occurred?

_____

_____

Connection with Source is essential for successful Visioning. Recall in the introduction of the last chapter where you declare your awareness of your Source; review that section.

5) **Controlling Our Thoughts**

When we Vision, we want to empty our cup, removing any prior ideas or thoughts we have about Visioning, including any prior attempts, whether successful or not. Be as completely open as you can, with no prior ideas about what you're doing. To do this we need to control our thoughts, which is essential for Visioning.

In the last chapter, the second key to enlightenment, *Beyond Duality/Beyond Time – One Who Is Free From the Pairs of Opposites and the Past, Present and Future,* is a guided meditation which will give you the grounding to control your thoughts to manifest your Vision.

Putting Visioning Into Practice

Below is an outline on how to use Visioning. It's designed to get you familiar with its "mechanics" by applying it to your daily life. We will explore how to apply Visioning to fulfill your dreams a little further in the section Visioning the Life you Desire, but for the time being this breakdown will help you master its aspects.

1) Desire

A Vision starts with an authentic desire. Start small; maybe it's the parking spot you want at the mall, your favorite produce at the grocery store, the product you want at the supermarket, getting to work on time when your late, or getting that right gift for your friend. Make your Vision something you authentically desire in the moment.

2) Your desire and imagination is more real than the world around you.

Know the Universe is an illusion. Consciousness is all there is, which makes your desire and imagination more real than the world around you.

3) Feel the fulfillment of the desire.

For your chosen Vision, what are you feeling when it has been fulfilled? Take your time to think this through. For example; feel the security that you found that parking spot. Feel the excitement that you found that produce to make that great meal. Feel your relaxation as you get to work on time.

Your feelings of the Vision fulfilled is a Being state, therefore ask yourself what are you Being? Then Be that now.

4) See the details in your imagination.

Make the effort to form the image and be specific about what it is you desire. See yourself in first or third person but see the detail. See the parking spot available, see the produce on the shelf, see yourself walking in your work with one minute to spare.

5) Your desire is the Universe's desire.

While producing the feelings, Being, and imagery of the future moment in the present, recall your connection to Source, and know that the Vision is known. You are the Source and your desire is its desire – feel that within. A level of awareness exists in which you can feel the Universe knows your desire.

Through the mechanism of cause and effect, it responds to your thoughts and feelings, copying what you Vision for it to produce.

When we hold that the Vision is known by our Source then we expect it, which only reinforces its creation. You're therefore not in any type of anxiety about it, you're not overthinking it, and you're not having any thoughts about it. Because when you expect, you're living in behaviours and thoughts that reflect that you expect. With those thoughts you're telling the Universe that you know you can rely on it and it responds accordingly.

6) Control the Mind

Don't fantasize about the Vision or wonder how it will become real, as doing so sends a message to the Universe that you're trying to control its manifestation. Relax and rely on the Universe, knowing it will manifest it. If your finding this challenging, use your meditation practice, get in touch with your Consciousness, and/or repeat Aham Brahmasmi.

Visioning in a Hurry

Sometimes in our daily life we get in a bind on the spot and quickly need the outcome to go our way.

The quick formula is;
1) Be the desired outcome
2) Imagine exactly what you want.
3) Don't think about the "how" or create opposing thoughts about your desire.

For example;
You're running to catch the bus - you feel the security of being on it, and in your imagination you feel it is the very next one.

Your car breaks down in the cold - you feel the security of the help from a road service person, and in your imagination you see them there in a timely manner.

Try yourself with possible binds that could occur in your daily life.

Bind:
_____
_____
_____

Desired Being:
_____
_____

Detailed imagination:

Bind:

Desired Being:

Detailed imagination:

Bind:

Desired Being:

Detailed imagination:

Visioning the Life You Desire: Part 1 - We Are Creator Beings

Now we will apply your ability to Vision to help you create the life you desire. Below we break up this section into three parts;

1) We Are Creator Beings; in which we explore how we are constantly creating through Consciousness.
2) Finding Your Purpose; providing exercises to find your purpose and align it with your values and Being State in preparation to manifest it as your Vision.
3) Building and Manifesting the Vision; in which we provide exercises to build your Vision and how to handle the mind to manifest it.

If reality is an illusion, the Universe is connected to each of us, we are all Gods, and we have the power to Vision, then what is the point of life? We who originate in no space and no time, manifest in space and time for one purpose - to create, just like Source, which we do, every moment of every second, with the purpose to experience the creative process of life.

You have the power to create the physical Universe, from your Being and thoughts. The more ignorant we are of this power, the more autopilot our life appears. The more aware we are, the more we witness the power of our thoughts - *Pragyanaam Brahma*; Consciousness creates reality. Consciousness creates physical reality, as in the circumstances and objects in your life. We create just like God creates, it just doesn't occur in the way in which we think. It is through our Being.

We but mirror the world. All the tendencies present in the outer world are to be found in the world of our body. If we could change ourselves, the tendencies in the world would also change. As a man changes his own nature, so does the attitude of the world change towards him. This is the divine mystery supreme. A wonderful thing it is and the source of our happiness.
-Mahatma Gandhi

The joy of Consciousness, your joy, is defining and creating your life, creating your experiences, and the creation of Self. We are creator Beings.

To help us understand how we are creating, below is a description of the tools of creation we use every moment of our lives.

Every thought we have, every word we utter, and every action we make are acts of creation that define our Self in the relative world of all choices. Can you see your own response to this sentence is a choice, and then that choice has defined you? But this is not all of our creative power; it is intention, Being state, and imagination which are our tools of creation to empower our physical lives with Consciousness. With all of these – thought, word, action, intention, Being state, and imagination – we are endlessly creating Self.

The most important to understand are the last three, and this is because within every experience we go through, every day of our lives, is an intention, Being state, and imagination. Below they are described in detail.

Intention – Every thought you produce has an intention. Every word uttered has an intention. And every action of your body as it moves through space and time starts with the impulse of intention. You get up to grab a cup of coffee; you have an intention to relax or energize yourself. You want to walk your dog; you have an intention to have a healthy dog. Your body is the sum of all your past intentions.

Being State - Every thought, word, and action is produced from a Being state. When you drive on a road trip with your partner what are you Being? When you have an interview for that new job what are you Being? Our Being state defines our present moment experience.

Imagination - As you think in time and space you visualize in pictures. Imagination is the eye of Consciousness. You want to go and hang out with friends; you may actually see the image of what you expect in your mind before you do. You need to go grocery shopping; you may actually see yourself shopping before you have gone. Your imagination projects the future.

When we are unconscious about our intentions, Being state, and imagination then our creative tools can be influenced by past information, false stories in our mind, or given to us from ideals in society, by our parents, or authority figures. The result is we will not create new experiences from our true authentic Self – from Consciousness.

When we are conscious of our creation in life we know our intention, what we are Being, and the images we are projecting in our imagination. This is living from Consciousness which creates new experiences for us, expanding our life.

Life is not about learning a philosophy or theory about our existence, but putting into practice and experiencing that we are creators. My teacher once shared a story that exemplifies this change of perspective called *The Man in the Mango Grove*;

There's a man who went to an orchard, a mango grove, to eat mangoes. When he went inside the mango grove he started making notes. He took out a pen and paper and started tabulating how many trees there were, how many leaves were growing in each, how many mangos would grow.

A gardener came upon this man inside the mango grove, the orchard, and said, "What are you doing? Why have you come here?"

He said, "I've come here to eat mangoes."

Perplexed, the gardener said, "So why don't you eat mangoes? Why do you have to tabulate how many trees are there, and how many leaves are growing, and how the mango grows? Why don't you eat the mango and enjoy yourself?"

The man said, "Ya, I forgot what I came here for." So, he put back his pencil and paper and enjoyed the mangoes to his contentment.

We come here on Earth to fulfill our heart with our ability to create, and instead, we get distracted by tabulating our lives like the fellow in the mango grove. We can end up focusing on wealth, recognition, or fleeting fulfillments of happiness. Not to moralize wealth and recognition, as they are great rewards when we live to our heart, but when they are our focus they rob us of our truth. Enriching our life with creation and choosing new experiences is the point.

The World of the Relative

If our Consciousness resides in the Absolute of space and time, then it exists in a realm where everything is completed, meaning there is nothing to experience because all experiences can be had at once.

If this is the state of God, living in completion in the Absolute, then the only way for God to experience anything is by creating an experience of separation, or illusioned separation. This is the purpose of the world of the relative, to create a state of illusioned separation. The world around us is the world of the relative; relative because everything exists in our world in a state of illusioned separation in relation to everything else, between anything and its opposite - up-down, male-female, happy-sad, here-there, hot-cold.

Right now, think of three traits of your character that define who you are and write them below. For example: kind, funny, empathic.

1)_____
2)_____
3)_____

Think how you came to know you are each of these traits. Sometimes it is in our teenage years where we learn who we like to Be. Maybe you were not that trait and then decided to become that trait at some point in your life, or maybe someone close to you showed you the value of being that trait. Whenever it is, if you can, bring that moment to mind.

Can you see how the world of the relative, the existence of the opposite of who you are, helped you make the choice to Be who you are.

The purpose of the relative world is to create an experience back to the Source so we don't just know that we are God, we experience that we are God, which we couldn't do if we remained in the Absolute. This movement back to the Source, that allows us to experience we are God, is the point - this evolution is the purpose of our lives here in the physical.

It is in relationship to other things that growth happens. I choose to experience peace because I have once experienced stress and anxiety. I choose to experience joy because I have once experienced pain. It is having a relationship to pain that made me seek an experience of joy. In the world of the Absolute, I would already be experiencing joy, but the creative love of my life is that I choose to create the experience, as opposed to just being in joy from birth. This isn't just for us individually but for us collectively as well.

The social system of health care started in Britain in response to the atrocities of World War 2. It was these atrocities that created the Consciousness of humanity not seen in history - providing free medical care for all. In a time of great human suffering humanity chose a great act of kindness. Acts like these define who humans are in times of hardship, the same way our own individual hardships define us. As we see the horrible things that humanity can do, know that these events help us create who we choose to Be, as a species, and as a global humanity.

If you don't see the power of fear and pain to make you successful then that fear and pain will become the poison of your life.
 -Maharaj

Let's do an exercise to see how our hardships were used by us to create ourselves. Take the three most negative events of your life. Be gentle and do your best while writing the event to be removed from any emotion of the pain. If you can, for this exercise, decide that it won't be painful.

Describe the negative events below. For example; got fired from my job.

1)

2)

3)

Now describe as objectively as you can what actually occurred, not about you, not about your emotion, but as a removed observer of the emotions. Just what actually happened, not how it affected you. For example; I told my boss months before that I didn't think this job was for me, he spent several months trying to get me to quit, before firing me.

1)

2)

3)

Now write down what resulted from the painful event. Not what happened emotionally, but in the larger picture of your life, what happened. For example; moved on and started my own business.

1)

2)

3)

The purpose of this exercise is to demonstrate that the events of our lives help us create who we choose to Be. Even out of the most painful events of our lives is a creation of Self. And we can approach all current problems in this creative way: who do I choose to Be in regard to this event.

What current pain in your life can you reframe as helping you define yourself? Who is it that you want to Be in regard to the scenario that is causing you pain? This is the question that guides me in my times of hardship, 'Who do I want to Be in regard to this event? It is this question that makes me consciously approach my challenges. We enrich our experience of Consciousness when we live conscious of our experience; of our intention, of what we are Being, and of the images we produce (i.e. the Vision) of the expected desire.

We Are the Vision of Our Higher Self

The events in our lives can sometimes come out of nowhere and change us forever. And sometimes they can be tragic or painful. Some people can be born into challenging circumstances. In these scenarios did these people create their reality?

Yes, but not in the way we think. The events that appear as "acts of God," in our life are creations of our own Higher Self. Knowing this helps us answer the question, "If I am creating my life are you telling me I created the car accident that made me a paraplegic?" or, "Are you saying I created my abuse?" and, "Are innocent children in war torn countries creating the atrocities that are happening to them?"

We should never hold an idea in our minds that the pain that has been caused from unfortunate circumstances, such as from atrocities or abuse, are directly created from thoughts such as, "I want to have an atrocity happen to me." Yet there is a level of creation beyond this life in which we do choose events for the purpose of our growth. This is the detached God level of the Higher Self.

For those "acts of God" that seem out of our control, the creation we are responsible for then is not *Why did I create this?* but instead, *Who do I choose to Be in response to this event?* When our pain has formed our lives, we cannot be told we created them, not consciously, or even unconsciously, but instead they were created in the level beyond this life, the level of our own Higher Self. Our pains are here to evolve us, to help us make choices out of the pain. The strength of mind and character that is created from choosing to love in response to pain is the type of circumstances the Higher Self puts us in.

You did create them, just not in the way we understand, and it does not benefit the experiencer of the pain to ask why did I create this, but instead *Who do I choose to Be in response to this?* And then use your ability to create consciously the life you desire in response to the pain.

Visioning the Life You Desire: Part 2 - Finding Your Purpose

When we live from purpose, we live from the power of our Consciousness. Therefore, to use Consciousness to Vision and manifest the life we desire we align it with our purpose.

Everyone wants to find their purpose, largely I believe because we imagine it will make living easy. Yet it will often be in the struggle and challenge of life, when we are up against the opposite of who we are, that we thirst the most to make meaning out of our life. At times we all may have felt purposelessness, and it can be our greatest pain, and this is because it does not speak to the truth of our soul.

As Creator Beings it is our nature to make meaning of our experience in the physical realm, yet our purpose is found in a paradox that life itself holds no purpose, no shoulds or should nots, no rules or plans, just experience and creation. Life is freedom, the feeling of free falling into a black abyss, and it is here where true purpose is found.

A story my teacher tells resembles the struggle we all have in finding our purpose;

In the dark, a person is thrown down into an abyss. He starts falling and at dawn he comes back from where he was thrown, that is the end of his life. His life is the fall throughout the night. As soon as he's thrown, he's grappling and looking for places to hold on. He's looking for tree branches or ledges, anything that he can grab onto, to hang on cause he does not know where he is going to fall too. It could be craggy rocks with scorpions and snakes and worms and leeches. He does not know whether he's going to fall into a marsh, he couldn't see anything. While falling he found a branch of a tree. This tree was growing on a cliff. He just grabbed onto that branch and clung on all night long. His arms were aching, tearing away from his body, but he still clung on. He did not know where he was going to fall if he let go. All night long he lived out his life in fear and found that branch very comforting. He found that pain to be worth going through even though his armpit was tearing apart. And as dawn came, the first light of day, he saw below his feet, not scorpions, not craggy rocks, not marshes with leeches in it, but he saw the most magnificent turf, grass blowing in the breeze, flowers all around. But it was too late, it was dawn, in that world the first light of day you have to return back from where you came. His eternal life ended.

This is how we live life, scared of the free fall, scared of the unknown, so we hold on in fear and find it comforting.

If we truly observe the objective reality of life then our purpose lies in the full freedom of making it as we want. The joy is actually feeling the complete creative freedom in making any purpose as we want while living here in time and space.

It all starts then in knowing that nothing has any meaning except the meaning we give it. All the events and people in your life have no meaning except that which you give it. Life is a playground of experience. Unfortunately, oftentimes the meaning we give something doesn't come from an authentic truth within us but from others around us.

It's in the clean slate of purposelessness that purpose can be found. Purpose isn't uncovered, it is a choosing; a direction we point in the infinite span of human experience. And that's often the point for us; the options are too vast. It's in fact not that we don't want to make a purpose, but that we don't want to risk our lives learning that what we chose as a purpose is not what we want. So we stay safe, willing to take the purpose given to us by our society, friends, or family, in hopes that we don't have to think about it for ourselves.

Neurologist and psychiatrist Viktor Frankl, author of the landmark book *Man's Search for Meaning* (1946), creator of logotherapy, believed finding purpose was central to the human motivational force and spent his years studying it. The research is clear: when we live with a purpose we create change in our own lives as well as in the lives of others, and it helps us remain positive even while surrounded by negative or painful circumstances.

Defining Purpose

Carl Jung believed within us was an intelligent, meaning-making subconscious that was reflected in our dreams and unconscious impulses. That dreams were the subconsciousness's way of trying to create a complete and whole self by showing us parts of ourselves that are unresolved. He believed embedded within all of us is a natural desire for a completed psyche.

I have always felt our individual purpose is the natural push within for a complete and whole humankind. That our search for a life of purpose is a natural impulse of our collective psyche, which helps bring wholeness to humanity. As dreams are to the individual, purpose is to the collective. By living out our purpose we help bring humanity to wholeness, make it more complete, to resolve unresolved issues in our collective psyche.

So, I define purpose as; <u>a conscious intention for your life, that, even in the smallest way helps bring humanity to wholeness, moves it forward, makes it more complete, or resolves unresolved issues in our collective psyche, and importantly, however this statement is interpreted by the individual.</u>

We don't all have to build the next supercomputer; if you think lollipops make people happy and that is your definition of moving the collective, then let it be your purpose to make lollipops.

Just as a dream can reveal a painful issue in your life that needs to be addressed, urging you to wholeness outside of your comfort zone, your purpose will also live outside your comfort zone. One of the reasons why people don't ever find a true purpose is because it is outside their comfort zone. Your purpose should make you uncomfortable. You can't make a difference to the collective by being comfortable; get fired, quit your job, end that poisonous friendship, move from that home, start that business, stand up in front of those people. Make the waves that your heart wants you to by living your purpose and moving the collective. The collective needs your purpose.

Finding Your Purpose?

It is here that I provide for you some exercises that I hope will help you find your purpose. I have used them with many people with great success.

Timeline Exercise

1) Placing a piece of paper sideways, preferable legal size, draw a long horizontal line. If that's not available, no problems, as any paper will do. Let this line represent your entire life until the present moment.
2) Note on the line important and pivotal points throughout your life. Describe why these events are important, and the meaning they made for you.
3) Now that you see a bird's eye view of your life and its defining events, use a coloured highlighter and highlight when passion was in your life. It could be anything you deem,

such as; when you were creative, or maybe something in your life gave you meaning. Note on your timeline what you were passionate about.
4) Using a different coloured highlighter highlight when in your life you felt you were at your best. Note on your timeline what you were doing that made you feel you were at your best.
5) Now take a minute to reflect on your timeline. What does it feel like to look at your life in this way? What have you noticed? What sticks out to you? Write here any reflections you have.

_____
_____
_____
_____
_____

6) Now do this meditation;

Close your eyes and take a deep breath through your nose and into your belly. Put your focus in between your eyebrows and see a white or blue dot. Say Pragyanaam Brahma five times....Think about your timeline...Feel your timeline...(10 sec)...Feel what you learned and what it feels like to see your life in this way...(10 sec)...Now see your life as a baby on your timeline...(20 sec)...See yourself as a child on your timeline...(20 sec)...See yourself as an adolescent on your timeline...(20 sec)...See your adult life on your timeline...(20 sec)...See the potential future, the mystery of what's to come on your timeline...(20 sec)...This is your life and not anyone else's. This is not your family's life, not your friend's life, not your job's life, though you share it with others, nobody else is your purpose. Only you experience your life, only you live your life. You can freely love and invite and share in your life with others, but only you live it...(10 sec)...Our time here is precious...what is it that you want to do with your time on this earth ...(5 sec)...Your life is precious...(10 sec)...Now, coming back to your timeline, see the part of your timeline that still has to be created. Now, we are going to take a trip into the future. See yourself at 80 years old...you've lived your life right to the end, right to the end of your life...What is missing?...(5 sec)...Is anything missing?...(5 sec)...Is there an unfulfillment somewhere?...What speaks to you?...What does your heart say is missing?...(5 sec)...What do you see?...(30 sec)...Now, come back to the present moment and feel the time you have left...If you are living your purpose in 5 years, what are you doing?...(20 sec)...If you are living your purpose in 10 years, what are you doing?...(20 sec)...If you are living your purpose in 20 years, what are you doing?...(20 sec)...What speaks to you?...What do you see?...What do you hear?...It may have spoken to you through your passion...or when you were at your best...or it speaks as a desired fulfillment for an experience you are seeking to have...(10 sec)...Now, breathe into your belly...Looking up at your third eye and feeling your heart ask, "What is my purpose?"...Make sure you don't force an answer, just notice if any feelings occur, or if any thoughts or images arise..."What is my purpose?"...(30 sec)...This time ask the question like you're asking a deep part of your Being, still with your focus on your third eye, "What is my purpose"...Again, make sure you don't force an answer, just notice if any feelings occur, or if any thoughts or images arise...(30 sec)...When you're ready, take one last deep breath and come back to the room.

7) Make notes and reflect on what you experienced.

_____
_____
_____
_____
_____
_____

Did that work for you? Most who try the above exercise find a direction to point their life. If not, no problem, finding your purpose can take time. Purpose is often speaking to you through passion, or moments when you are at your best. If the above exercise didn't work for you, try spending time answering the following questions.

Exercise 2 - Questions to Contemplate Your Purpose

Answer these questions privately or meditate on them. Let them percolate inside you as they may draw an answer your looking for.

- Have you ever had a dream that stays with you for years?
- Have you ever had the thought *This is it?*
- What are you willing to die for?
- What has your heart never experienced before that it would like to?
- What makes you love life?

If you're still stuck finding your purpose, no problem, it takes time. I recommend still choosing something that you can label a "temporary" purpose for the time being, as it is important to consciously choose a direction in life. You can always change your purpose.

What have you chosen as your purpose?

My purpose is;

_____

_____

Aligning Your Values with Your Purpose

In the words of Mahatma Gandhi:

> *Your beliefs become your thoughts*
> *Your thoughts become your words*
> *Your words become your actions*
> *Your actions become your habits*
> *Your habits become your values*
> *Your values become your destiny*

We come into this world not knowing who we are, why we are here, and where we are going from here. Our lack of direction can make us feel like we are on a boat, drifting on the ocean without any direction. Our purpose then becomes the island which we can see out on the vast ocean. Our values are the equipment of our boat that get us there, such as the rudder, sail and engine. While our Vision is the wind that blows in our direction towards our purpose; the forces that appear beyond our control, which we don't perceive as being a part of us.

After we have declared our purpose, we align it with our values. Values are those principles which we deem important to ourselves and become reflected in our actions. When we are conscious of our values, and are moving towards them in our life, we are happy.

Take a look at this list of values and circle or write down in a journal or notebook those with which you would say are you resonate with. Don't think about it too much, just let your heart in the present moment guide your process.

1. Acceptance/self-acceptance: to be accepting of myself, others, life, etc.
2. Adventure: to be adventurous; to actively explore novel or stimulating experiences.
3. Assertiveness: to respectfully stand up for my rights and request what I want.
4. Authenticity: to be authentic, genuine, and real; to be true to myself.
5. Caring/self-care: to be caring toward myself, others, the environment, etc.
6. Compassion/self-compassion: to act kindly toward myself and others in pain.
7. Connection: to engage fully in whatever I'm doing and be fully present with others.
8. Contribution and generosity: to contribute, give, help, assist, or share.
9. Cooperation: to be cooperative and collaborative with others.
10. Courage: to be courageous or brave; to persist in the face of fear, threat, or difficulty.
11. Creativity: to be creative or innovative.

12. Curiosity: to be curious, open-minded, and interested; to explore and discover.
13. Encouragement: to encourage and reward behaviour that I value in myself or others.
14. Excitement: to seek, create, and engage in activities that are exciting or stimulating.
15. Fairness and justice: to be fair and just to myself or others.
16. Fitness: to maintain or improve or look after my physical and mental health.
17. Flexibility: to adjust and adapt readily to changing circumstances.
18. Freedom and independence: to choose how I live and help others do likewise.
19. Friendliness: to be friendly, companionable, or agreeable toward others.
20. Forgiveness/self-forgiveness: to be forgiving toward myself or others.
21. Fun and humor: to be fun loving; to seek, create, and engage in fun-filled activities.
22. Gratitude: to be grateful for and appreciative to myself, others, and life.
23. Honesty: to be honest, truthful, and sincere with myself and others.
24. Industry: to be industrious, hardworking, and dedicated.
25. Intimacy: to open up, reveal, and share myself, emotionally or physically.
26. Kindness: to be kind, considerate, nurturing, or caring toward myself or others.
27. Love: to act lovingly or affectionately toward myself or others.
28. Mindfulness: to be open to, engaged in, and curious about the present moment.
29. Order: to be orderly and organized.
30. Persistence and commitment: to continue resolutely, despite problems or difficulties.
31. Respect/self-respect: to treat myself and others with care and consideration.
32. Responsibility: to be responsible and accountable for my actions.
33. Safety and protection: to secure, protect, or ensure my own safety or that of others.
34. Sensuality and pleasure: to create or enjoy pleasurable and sensual experiences.
35. Sexuality: to explore or express my sexuality.
36. Skillfulness: to continually practice and improve my skills and apply myself fully.
37. Supportiveness: to be supportive, helpful, and available to myself or others.
38. Trust: to be trustworthy; to be loyal, faithful, sincere, and reliable.
39. Other_____
40. Other_____

Source: The Illustrated Happiness Trap (Harris & Aisbett, 2014)

To help us narrow down your top values we are going to use your past experiences.

Recall a time in your life when you were happy. Describe this time here.

In detail, why were you happy?

What values were involved with your happy time?

Recall a time in your life when you were fulfilled or satisfied. Describe this time here.

In detail, why were you fulfilled?

What values were involved with your moment of satisfaction?

Recall a time when you experienced a sense of purpose. Describe this time here.

In detail, what drove your sense of purpose?

What values were involved with your sense of purpose?

_____

_____

_____

Now, after looking at your list, and seeing which values contributed to your happiness, fulfillment, and purpose, write down those that repeated themselves or that stood out to you. Write them here as your top five values.

1)_____

2)_____

3)_____

4)_____

5)_____

Notice the feelings you have doing this exercise. If you have positive feelings, maybe a warmth, this is love of your spirit that gets its joy from defining itself in the world of the relative.

In our life as humans we have only one job; we define...Every time you define you limit and that is the enjoyment, that is creation.
 -*Maharaj*

Now that we have identified your top five values we want to move to actualizing them as experiences that move us towards our purpose.

Being Your Values

Now that we have identified your top five values, choose those top three which speak most to your purpose. Here we will turn them into Being states.

Name your value #1.

_____

Now name the Being state your value represents. For example, compassion is Being compassionate, and acceptance is Being accepting.

_____

Now add your I am to your Being state. For example, I am Being compassionate.

_____

Now close your eyes and focus on your heart and try to Be, right now, the Being state. This may take time. If you need to, remember a time when you were that Being state and experience it again. Feel it fully if you can but don't force it. Just open yourself to experiencing your chosen Being state.

Name your value #2.

_____

Now name the Being state your value represents.

_____

Now add your I am to your Being state.

_____

Again, close your eyes, focus on your heart, and try to Be, right now, the Being state. And again, feel it fully if you can but don't force it. Just open yourself to experiencing your chosen Being state.

Name your value #3.

_____

Now name the Being state your value represents.

_____

Now add your I am to your Being state.

_____

Again, close your eyes and focus on your heart and try to Be, right now, the Being state. And again, feel it fully if you can but don't force it. Just open yourself to experiencing your chosen Being state.

    Now go about living your life as normal but come from your chosen Being state. Maybe set a reminder mid-day, and then see what you're compelled to do, what is drawn to you, or how the Universe responds.
    The Being state creates the unfolding magic of our lives.

Visioning the Life You Desire: Part 3 - Building and Manifesting the Vision

There is great joy in giving ourselves the liberty to believe in our grandest dream and to live out a life that we desire. For some people it doesn't feel natural to dream big and that is OK. Yet we all desire to live a fulfilled life, and we all seek to love and be loved through the impact of our community. Unconsciously this manifest as desires for wealth and fame, and there is nothing wrong with these as they are natural. Visioning the fulfillment of these desires is therefore natural.

It could almost appear selfish to desire big, to dream large, yet this type of self-love is the love of Source. If it feels good to experience, then Source agrees, and we can all agree; having and spending money feels good, and having community respect feels good.

How do you have larger thoughts than you're capable of believing? By believing that imagination is more important than the world around you. If you believe the physical world is more relevant than your Consciousness you will always believe that larger dreams that seem unachievable are beyond you and foolish to imagine. But if you're aware that the only thing that keeps such things from you, is your imagination, then the door opens for you to experiencing them.

This here is a meditation to expand your imagination;

Sit in your meditation posture, close your eyes, and take a few deep breaths into your diaphragm.

Now visualize yourself on a grassy plateau on a mountain. It is beautiful there, with a warm gentle breeze, there are other mountains around you, take in this majestic landscape....See little mountain flowers at your feet...bend down and smell one...what does it smell like....stand up again...and as you do you see a cabin sized square structure not far from you...It is clearly a small building but is perfectly square....Walk over to this structure with curiosity. As you approach you see a door and a computer panel....Then the structure communicates to you and says, "You have been given the opportunity to experience a holographic room, a virtual reality room, a place where you can program another world, and it will look and feel real. In this room you can program anything that you want to experience, with only one condition - the experience has to be connected to your life's purpose in any way you feel." This is the room of your life's purpose...Don't make it based on money, or what you can earn, simply feel the limitlessness of your opportunity....As you stand outside this structure, what do you choose...Have fun...Know that you can walk into this room and experience being a rock star being adored by thousands of fans in a stadium...or the head of an international company selling products you come up with......or maybe you just want to experience what it is like to be at the bottom of the ocean, as long as it is connected to your purpose.....Be creative...Allow this opportunity to stretch your mind...You can even make something up that doesn't exist. Feel the limitlessness. If you have trouble choosing, then just break the rules and choose whatever experience you want to."

See the door to this room and the control panel. Now you have to program your world. The language of this computer is thought and feeling. Being by telling the computer what feeling you are looking to fulfill with your creation. Take a moment to think this through. Put words to the feelings.

Now with your virtual reality 'life purpose' room programmed we will open the door counting down from three...3...2...1. Open the door and walk into your purpose.

Observe what you are seeing and feeling. See the details. Let whatever scenario you created play out...

(2-4 min)

Now it is time to leave your virtual reality purpose world. Enjoy what you have seen and know you can always come back. Turn around and walk out the door you came in on and experience gratefulness for this moment that you could have this experience. Feel the gratitude. Now as you are back on the mountain plateau, look out and see the beautiful scenery. You are done here. Now gently let this image fade away.

Take one last deep breath, bring your hands to the ground and open your eyes.

What did you program in the computer? What feelings were you looking to fulfill? What details did you see? Write your answers below.

_____
_____
_____
_____
_____
_____

Now that you have unleashed a Vision of your purpose, flush out the details.

When is this Vision? When is it taking shape?

_____
_____
_____

Where is your Vision taking place? What is the city or type of environment?

_____
_____
_____

What are you doing? What takes up your days?

_____
_____
_____

Who do you see yourself surrounded by? What type of people?

_____
_____
_____

Spend a moment being grateful for the manifestation of your Vision. Even though you might not see it physically, it is there.

Preparation for Visioning

The purpose of the last exercise is to get you better at expanding your imagination. You can use the Vision of your purpose for the below steps, but they are laid out for any Vision you choose, from a new relationship, career, car, smartphone -whatever you desire.

Limitation of Resources Is a State of Mind

The only way we can exist as Creator Beings is by knowing we have the same power Source does; the power of creation out of nothing. If we are Creator Beings, co-creating with Source, and Source is the unlimited unmanifested Universe, then our potential in relying on Source is also unlimited. When we understand that Source is on our side and expresses unlimited potential in us, that experience becomes a part of our lives. The identity of the Consciousness is unleashed, because that is where the Consciousness resides, in a place of unlimited potential.

If the creation of our Universe is happening now, then any limitation of resources is a state of mind. This one is hard to hear. Haven't we been fighting all our lives for resources; money, time, love, sex, stuff, and lots of different stuff.

One of our biggest challenges with Visioning is the perceived race to get what we want. A belief that the thing we desire is hard to get or is limited. We feel that if we are to Vision for a job there are only a limited number of them out there, then our Visioning becomes created out of scarcity or poverty Consciousness. This thought is a creative act which says there are limited resources to produce your Vision, which the Universe will simply produce for you as an experience. Think about it; if you actually believed in your ability to Vision then you would not be concerned about the resources to create it, they would be in fact unlimited, as unlimited as your ability to imagine the resources. It may be hard to believe but try. Let the resources of the thing you're Visioning be unlimited. Any thought you have created about any limitation of resources is you simply creating thoughts that choose to limit.

I have had wild magical manifestations occur from not believing the words of those around me. *Wow it's really hard getting a job in that field*, or, *You probably won't find a place to rent in that area*. I never believed the limits placed upon me, and lived completely that the resources of the things I wanted were unlimited. You can to.

So goes the ancient Vedic line from the Upanishads;

That is Infinite. This is Infinite. From that Infinite arises This Infinite. This Infinite is brought forth from That Infinite and That Infinite remains Infinite.
  -Isha Upanishad

This line boggles the mind of the untrained reader, but contemplate on this. This is how the Universe exists; in infinite resources of creation in the present. In creation, this is how to manifest the things that you want. The thing with which you desire to manifest, have no thought of how hard or challenging it is. Live in the unlimited infinite of all that you desire.

Say out loud the words *It is unlimited*. Whatever the thing with which you believe is limited, say out loud that it is unlimited. Whatever the thing you're Visioning, whatever the thing with which you think makes you happy or defines your happiness, there is enough of it in the world, it is unlimited. You will be surprised how much with which you don't need when you feel there is enough of the things you desire.

You Created Your Present Circumstances So Accept Them

If we are One with our world then are not the events, circumstances, and conditions that affect us simply reflections of our Self in Unity with All things?

Your circumstances should not make you; they only show you what you were. Your circumstances do not make you, you make your circumstances.
  -Tulshi Sen; Ancient Secrets of Success

If there is something in your life you don't like, this is you calling this aspect of Source into your life. Life observes cause and effect, and we are using our Source power to call upon ourselves whatever we choose.

As a part of Visioning it is important to accept and not judge the reality you are in now, because you created it. If you're running from your current reality, then you're running from a part of yourself. As well, you're giving the message to the Universe that you are the victim of your circumstances, which is the exact opposite mind frame required to Vision. You are the owner of your circumstances, so the reality is, you're deciding to create something new.

Engage Your Source

You cannot ever miss your mark when you are one with your Consciousness.
   -Tulshi Sen; Ancient Secrets of Success

That Visioning sounds too good to be true is why it is the gift of love, joy, and compassion of the Universe. Your desire is not separate from the Universe. It is the Universe desiring what you desire, with no thought, or judgment about it. The same way the galaxies spin, and animals exist, and the clouds rain; your Vision is simply a part of the Universe.

You are God, feel it, embrace it as your identity - Aham Brahmasmi. You have all the creative power that God has. You are simply a smaller version of it. The Universe is Consciousness; therefore it is aware of the present Being state that you are experiencing, that you are projecting.

Realize that you are that God that you have heard of all your life, having been inside you and sharing in your experiences. This is repeated in Herme's dictum, *As the Macrocosm so the Microcosm and as the Microcosm so the Macrocosm.*

In your Unity you realize it isn't just you desiring but God in you desiring. Can you conceive that the feeling of the Vision inside you is God inside you. This shared experience than assures you that the Universe knows of your desire and is working with you to manifest it. The Conscious Universe knows of the Vision. This shared experience is truly the joy of existence - that what you desire, God desires.

Contemplate your omnipresence. You are one with it all, right now wherever you are. Your Unity with all that is is your security for the manifestation of your Vision. Meditate on this. Feel this now. You are One with All things. Your omnipresence with the entire Universe is the point of it all. And this is the best way to manifest your Vision, knowing and experiencing your omnipresence with All.

Visioning is the power of your true nature, therefore to make it work properly you have to be your true nature which as a piece of the One.

The Vision

Tools of Creation

1. **Intention**

What is the intention of the creation? Why do you desire what you desire?

_____

_____

There have been plenty of times when I started a Vision but wasn't clear that my Being wasn't feeling it. When that happens, you will have trouble manifesting it, so here is an extra step to add clarity.

Does the desire for the Vision come from your heart? If need be, feel the center of your Being. Be in meditation and feel your thoughts about your Vision. Ask the core of your Being, *Is this a Vision of my Being?*

Can you answer below if the intention is intrinsic or extrinsic, driven from internal desire or in response to external circumstances?

_____

_____

2. **Being State**

To manifest our Vision we need to create it in the Absolute, the space of no place and no time. The Absolute is more real than the place you call reality. The Absolute, the place of no time and space within you, that is your Being state. What is the Being state of the Vision already accomplished? Take your time as it requires mental effort to experience something in the future as if it's happening now, and to contemplate what that feels like. Make the effort and don't move forward until you have done this. You may have more than one Being state in your Vision so there are multiple lines. Write it here;

I am Being

_____

I am Being

_____

I am Being

_____

Your Vision in the Absolute is occurring in the now, and has a direct effect on the manifested physical Universe around you. Remember there is no time, so the Vision is more real than the present right now. With concentration you should be able to touch and taste the differences in space and time between your Vision and the physical realm around you. Feel that in your heart.

3. **Imagination**

Paint the picture of your Being state. What do you see? What do you see yourself doing? What do you see yourself having? See the details of the Vision already accomplished. Below is an outline to help you engage your senses in the imagination.

What do you see?

What do you hear?

What do you smell?

Actions of Creation

Every thought, word spoken, and action is creative. They are descriptive about what you believe and what you know.

Thinking: If the Vision was already accomplished how would you be thinking differently than you are now?

Speaking: How would you be speaking differently?

Doing: What would you be doing differently?

Live in your Vision by thinking how you would be thinking, saying what you would be saying, and doing what you would be doing if it already manifested. Do these things and do them often.

Living in the Vision

You do not need to leave your room. Remain sitting at your table and listen. Do not even listen, simply wait, be quiet, still and solitary. The world will freely offer itself to you to be unmasked, it has no choice, it will roll in ecstasy at your feet. The nonexistent is what we have not sufficiently desired.
  - *Franz Kafka*

Live in the Being state of the Vision as if it's already accomplished. Connect with the Universe and know that It knows your Being state.

Once you've placed the Vision in the Being state do not think about what you need to do to accomplish the Vision. That sends a message to the Universe that you will try and manifest it yourself instead of relying on It to do so.

Instead, think about what the fun thing to do is, or what are you compelled to do from your feelings - not from your mind, but from your heart. Enjoy life. You could be in a coffee shop but feeling the Absolute with your Vision fulfilled. If you're in stressed times and are Visioning its solution, then you're going to look very relaxed on the outside when others would expect you to be panicking. By Being relaxed, your message to the Universe is your Being state, and therefore Vision, are the present moment.

It is not a future event; it happens at the same time. If the Absolute is real then when you create it, that's it, it's done. That's the real Creation, the more that is believed, the greater will the manifestation be. And this is how it works; it is existing Now in the Absolute.

Tips to Help Manifest the Vision

Love - Love the thing with which you Vision, and love your Vision. You attract that which you love. And love life while Visioning. Remain positive. Love the process of the manifestation of your Vision, as it is the reason you come here to the physical realm.

Gratefulness - Be grateful for the Vision already accomplished. When you're grateful you are saying, *the manifestation of my vision exists and I am grateful for it*. When you're grateful for it you send a message to the Universe that you know the Vision is already accomplished.

Expectation/Knowing - Expect your Vision, but in your heart, not in your mind. If you expect it in your heart, you know you are going to experience it, and it is in knowing that the Vision is accomplished. This is different from believing as belief contains a sliver of doubt, while knowing is a certainty, and the Universe responds accordingly. If you can't know, then you believe with an open non-judgmental mind, curious, with a desire to know.

Knowing is the declaration of truth, and to the degree it is known as truth is the degree it is made manifest.

Be Detached - Be detached from your Vision. If you are fully living in your Vision then you would not be tense or anxious for anything to occur, as you know it is going to happen. Any type of mental attachment produces a thought to the Universe that, right now, you do not experience your Vision.

Refrain From Fantasizing - Before or after Visioning, and while waiting for it to manifest, refrain from fantasizing about things with which you know you don't want to create. Visioning is a creative act of materialization with your thoughts, which you tell the Universe to listen to. When we fantasize out of habit we tell the Universe that you don't believe in the power of our thoughts to manifest.

Utilize Light -

The Universe creates and communicates through light, which contains intuitive data, data packets, and information. Pure light and its spectrums of colour is therefore one of the base intuitive information building mechanisms of the Universe, both spiritually and physically.
    -*The Mystic Book*

Sounds silly but shroud your Vision in golden light as I have found it assists in manifesting.

Under Your Pillow - Try writing out the entire Vision on a piece of paper and then place it under your pillow. Before you go to sleep Vision all the feelings as if they are present moment experiences.

Handling the Mind to Manifest Your Vision

We are so used to living from our mind and reacting to the physical world that it may seem challenging to rely on a Vision. There have been many times that I have saved my neck by manifesting a desire in stressful times. I'm quite experienced in keeping my calm when the outside world looks like it's falling apart. Yet it's at this time that negative thoughts can be the worst.

We all have mental habits or tendencies that can work against our manifestation. Here is some guidance on how to help control our mind as we wait for the Vision to manifest.

You now need to reject any negative thoughts that speak against your Vision. Literally, don't let yourself have them, at all. Feel the Being state and live in the creative energy which is your desire.

If you fall into a trap of your mind and have negative thoughts, literally tell the Universe *Cancel, cancel, cancel*. Replay the moment that just occurred in your imagination, that made you succumb to negative thinking, and see yourself instead thinking the positive thought, the expected thought, or the Being State, or the Vision. Literally replay the moment and see the positive thinking you wish you did instead. When you have even the slightest negative thought you have to put in the mental effort and change it. This requires vigilance of our thinking.

Likewise, never create anxiety that you had a negative thought. Instead, use your connection to the Source and ask for it not to manifest any negative thoughts.

Try not to have fear when Visioning, even if you're on the line. God is with you; you are the Universe. Know that if you can conquer this negative thinking will be better at handling other similar challenges. When you have a negative thought, simply think again and change the thought. Remember that the strength of meditation is in having the mind wander and then bringing it back. The strength is built by having resistance. Same with Visioning, you build mental strength when you turn your negative thought to a positive thought that supports your Vision.

Do not engage in how - Try not to have any thoughts, whatsoever about how to make your Vision manifest. Do what you're compelled to do through feeling, but not from your mind. By thinking about how to fulfill your Vision with your mind you immediately give the creative thought to the Universe that you don't want or need it to take care of the Vision for you. Try not to think about how your Vision will come to you. This is the challenge and why a relationship with the Source is needed; to have faith that your Being state and Vision are imprinting onto physical reality.

This was brought up in the Being State section in chapter two, and applies to Visioning, and it is about how we are conditioned to getting the things we want – by doing to Being. We are conditioned that if we want to Be something we have to do something first; I want to Be happy therefore I'll do something that makes me happy. But this is not how we manifest our Vision. Instead, we need to reframe and Be the thing we desire first, then "do" by going about our daily lives as normal and letting the Universe take over, either within or through guidance (synchronicities) outside of us. In the manifestation of your Vision there truly is an experience of *Let go and let God*. If you are recognizing the creative ability of your thoughts then don't think about the how, as it interferes with the process.

Meditate - Meditation helps you rely on Consciousness/Source to manifest your Vision. Do not forget to meditate on the Proclamation. Meditation keeps you in the reality that your true identity lives in the place where your Vision was formed. The quieting of the mind and the peace created by the Proclamation provides the anchor of your true identity as a Creator Being to Manifest the Vision.

The ultimate truth about relying on the Vision is that to do so we rely on the heart. It is about letting go of the mind in knowing that it could never conceive of the Vision, only the heart can.

You are important enough - Visioning is only possible when a change has occurred within that tells you *I am important, I have the power of the Universe on my side, I can create impact*. That is a profound philosophical change for most people and it can only happen when we look at ourselves and believe in a power like Source; the power of an aware Universe that is supporting us. Then we can make the change in our minds that when I Vision I don't have to think about the how, it will just occur. It is a shared experience of Unity.

An affirmation – While waiting for the Vision to manifest you can experience illusioned rejection, or the perceived opposite of your creation, and it can be helpful to repeat an affirmation to combat the minds tendency to fall for negative thoughts in those moments. Create a simple one-liner that contains exactly what you desire to create, such as, *I desire to be successful*, and use it in those times of doubt.

Learning From the Manifestation of a Vision

How the Vision manifests is an amazing opportunity to discover just how your thoughts, feelings, and Being impacts the physical world.

A Vision can manifest exactly as you saw it – yes, exactly as you saw it. This has occurred to me when I approached Visioning with the purist heart, and with the awe and wonder of a child. Yet it is not uncommon for the Vision to manifest without an important detail that was not considered in the imagination.

For example, I once met someone who Visioned winning the lottery. In their Vision they focused on the winning numbers and not on the emphasis of what it would feel like to Be living their life in the winnings. Lo and behold, their lottery numbers went up on the week they forgot to play.

Also, I knew of a woman who Visioned wealth by holding and counting money, then several months later she became a bank teller only to realize it was the manifestation of her Vision. She did not emphasize her Being on owning the money herself.

Visioning the detail is important.

What if after all your effort and patience your Vision doesn't manifest? This is the perfect time to reflect on the intention of the Vision. Possibly, your Higher Self has its own plans for you, or the Universe may have something else in store. Search your feelings. At this point you can even ask the Universe a straight question; *Why can't I materialize my Vision*. Listen to your Being, feeling, dreams or any synchronicities for an answer.

Sometimes it takes time to manifest your Vision. Let's say you want to change careers to become a writer. You create a Vision, then join a writing group, when out of nowhere the leader of the group retires and liking your enthusiasm asks you to take over. Now you're in a networking position but it's not the fruition of your Vision as you're not getting paid. This could be part of the path of its manifestation. If this is the case don't give up.

Visioning truly is the magic of the living Universe. Take advantage of your ability, as it is yours to experience, play with, and fulfill your heart.

Other Uses for Visioning

The Life Pie Exercise

This exercise was adapted from Julia Cameron's book the *Artist's Way (1992)*. Draw a circle on a piece of paper and then divide it into six pieces of pie. Label one pie spirituality, another exercise, another play, and so on, with work, friends, romance, and adventure. Place a dot in each slice at the degree to which you are fulfilled in that area (outer rim indicates great; inner circle, not so great). Then connect the dots. This will show you where you are lopsided. Whichever is the most, adapt the above exercises to build a Vision of what it looks like to fulfill that piece a pie. What is your Being if that part of your pie is fulfilled. What are you thinking, saying, and doing?

Visioning Emotional States

Take control of your day and how you want to react to the events in your life by Visioning the emotions you desire in the moment. Here are some examples;

Have to discuss a stressful report with your boss - Vision the pleasant feelings of you walking away from his office after a calm meeting between you too.

Feel overwhelmed with work - Vision your self midday laughing carefree with a friend, unaffected by the feelings of being overwhelmed.

You want to have a good day but you experienced emotional hardship earlier in the morning – Vision yourself feeling great and forgetting the hardship.

Experienced an emotional trauma in the past – Vision yourself not being triggered by it in the moment.

Using Visioning to Heal Past Life Pain

We choose our next world through what we learn in this one. Learn nothing, and the next world is the same as this one, all the same limitations and lead weights to overcome.
 - Sullivan, Jonathan Livingston Seagull

Karma simply means action, and being trapped in Karma means that all our actions are a ripple effect of our previous actions. It is an endless chain of the same conditions and it appears there is no escape from its iron grip.
  - Tulshi Sen; Ancient Secrets of Success

The tendencies acquired by a soul during a lifetime do not get lost with it. They are carried in a potential form for further development in births yet to come.
  - Swami Chidbhavananda, commentary on the Bhagavad Gita

We have planned this life and we have planned all of our lives. Taking the tendencies we have created from past lives, we then tweak our current life to either develop helpful ones or evolve out of harmful ones, by creating the world around us through thought and Being. The real you isn't even the you that experiences all the lives, the real you is the one that is planning them all.

On the level of the embodied Higher Self you know each life was designed to present challenges to further develop you. A pain in one life can be a blessing in another. But these pains were very real for our past life, just as the ones we create in this life now.

After doing the exercises in the chapter on the dimensionality of Consciousness, in which we explored past life awareness, you may have come across past life pain.

If you choose to work through the emotions then I recommend seeking out a licensed regression therapist.

The exercise below is not designed to replace the need to move through any latent past life emotions. If you feel that is required then seek that help first, otherwise you can try this exercise.

Once you have labeled the pain that was created in your past life, then identify the lack. For example, if the pain is humiliation, then the lack would be self-love. If it was loss of family then the lack would be family love. Whatever you found to be the lack in your past life pain, make a Vision to experience its fulfillment now. For example, with a lack of self-love, then make a Vision to experience self-love. Use the exercises from this chapter; discover the Being state, notice the images that come to mind, and how you would be thinking, speaking, and acting with your Vision fulfilled.

This healing is eternal healing. When the past life pain is the motivation of the Vision, true healing occurs.

Disentangling From the Stories that Control Us

On a daily basis we have thoughts that engross us. We go shopping, run errands, cook for the family, but our minds are occupied, drifting off somewhere else. It's often easier to control our mind when we are aware of the story that is controlling it.

Below are a list of themes that may engross us, or we may obsess over, or which occupy our mind. Circle the three most important themes which you feel occupy your mind.

Independence
Intellectual accomplishment
Self-criticism
Addictions
Overspending
Underearning
Security
Resistance to authority
Emotional dramas
Fear
Control
Gaining approval
Conformity
Family entanglements
Physical image
Lack of love
Anger
Guilt
Perfectionism
Revenge
Other

How have these themes added to or inhibited your life?

_____
_____
_____
_____
_____
_____

Now below see the new Vision for your old story;

Independence = Interdependence
Intellectual accomplishment = Wisdom
Self-criticism = Acknowledgment of Strengths
Addictions = Self-security
Overspending = Healing deprivation
Underearning = Being paid what you are worth

Security = Adaptability
Resistance to authority = Sharing leadership
Emotional dramas = Self-actualization
Fear = Love
Control = Trust
Gaining approval = Self trust
Conformity = Creativity
Famiy entanglements = Honest commitments
Physical image = Intrinsic worth
Lack of love = Divine love within
Anger = Empowerment
Guilt = Love with wisdom
Perfectionism = Self-acceptance
Revenge = Forgiveness
(*Adapted from the Celestine Prophecy: An Experiential Guide, Redfield and Adrienne, 1995*)

Can you see how each theme is a story created from root thoughts developed over your own history? The way out of these engrained stories is to Vision what you desire and rely on the Vision. Below is an outline to help you create your Vision from your themes, but if you want to expand on these you can adapt them to the previous exercises in this chapter.

Old Theme
_____

New Vision
_____

Name a Being State for your new Vision.
_____

Describe here how you would be thinking, speaking, and acting differently in your Vision.
_____
_____
_____
_____
_____
_____

Old Theme

_____

New Vision

_____

Name a Being State for your new Vision.

_____

Describe here how you would be thinking, speaking, and acting differently in your Vision.

_____
_____
_____
_____
_____
_____

Old Theme

_____

New Vision

_____

Name a Being State for your new Vision.

_____

Describe here how you would be thinking, speaking, and acting differently in your Vision.

_____
_____
_____
_____
_____
_____

Healing the Body

    As mentioned previously, our body responds to Visioning, so it can be used as a tool to explicate bodily healing. If you have endured a broken bone, sprained a muscle, or cut yourself, while healing, Vision the injured body part being used fully. See in your imagination yourself freely using the limb or injured body part as if there was no injury. If consistent enough you will notice the expedited healing.

The Completed State

We are true God selves, portions of the All, as affirmed when we experience that what we have Visioned on the inside becomes manifested reality on the outside. In truth because there is no inside or outside, as all is One. We become assured of our identity as God's manifested in individuality that are loving the separation and seeking joy in the Unity.

It is through experiencing Visioning that we can understand that Consciousness exists in a state of non-lack. When we live in a state where everything we desire can be fulfilled, and we are connected to All, then we never lack. Confidence in the fulfillment of the Vision creates detachment. Detachment is Karma Yoga which declares, *of myself I do nothing, the Source that dwells in me does all the work.*

The entire secret of Being is in detachment to your environment, to your friends and relatives and family, expressed in the line *My Self is the Self in all Beings*. This is the completed state in which you see your Being in all others, and you know your desires are fulfilled. '

This is the completed state Visioning awakens us to.

Brahman is complete and infinite. There is no lack in infinity. If there is no lack, there cannot be any desire. You can't say on one hand I am Brahman, Aham Brahmashmi, and then on the other hand you have wants and lacks. That is a contradiction in terms.

If you do have the desire, you live in its completed state, and the Universe complies. This is the grand state of knowing everything is meant to be, and everything happens in time and for a reason. You rely on and trust in the Universe.

This search outside for happiness is kama. The grabbing modification of the mind is kama. The waves and ripples on the surface of water obscure the sight of the sand bed below. The ripples of kama in the mind obstruct the vision of Atman...When the mind is pacified by relinquishing all the kamas, the blissful Atman is realized in Its original glory. He is a Brahma-jnani who intuits that the happiness he sought for in the world outside, is in its entirety in himself. He remains Self-satisfied.

-Swami Chidbuvananda, Commentary on the Bhagavad Gita

When the desires of the heart are satisfied, then you can be still within. And you awaken to the sport of life that is *leela*.

There Is No Rising

Welcome to the Embodiment of the Higher Self

There is no subconscious as there is nothing below.

There is no Higher Self as there is nothing higher

There is no Rising as the Absolute contains all culminations Now.

You may experience enlightenment but you can never say you are enlightened.
This way you do not seek any recognition for it, nor can you judge another for believing they are not it.
Treat everyone as if they are God,
as Brahman but in the process of realizing.

If any of the above does not make sense then do not continue.
Why?
Because the mind has to understand a Universe with duplicities and dichotomies,
where riddles and mysteries thrive,
having it be boggled and bewildered,
which lays the foundation to go beyond it,
Reread the earlier chapters until these above statements are true for you.

To Continue It Is Important To:

<u>Not have anger</u> - Do not blame anyone for anything in your life or your conditions. If you do, revisit chapter three and seven.

<u>Refrain from sexual activity for the period of this exercise</u> - This is not a judgment of morality. The energy of your Rising is latent in the base of the spine while sexual activity keeps it there. It's not going to harm you if you do engage in sexual activity during this exercise, you just might experience an imbalance of energy which would go away after meditating on the Hamsa. Try holding off from engaging in sexual activity until after a day from completing this exercise.

<u>Be detached</u> - Be detached from the little things. This doesn't mean you can't engage with them, but everything is a play of God and you can Vision anything you want.

<u>Commit</u> - Commit to God, commit to your Higher Self, commit to your spirit. Make the commitment. Do a ritual, whatever that means to you.

Do these next exercises only when you have made the commitment to light, to the white brotherhood, to all the ancient purity of master's that have come before us, to all those who expressed love in its purest form. Commit to that Higher Self, commit to that God.

You are God, so you are committing to yourself.

The Bhagavad Gita is a powerful display of love of the Master, the love of Source. The disciple sings;

> *Brahman is my Goal,*
> *my Total Support,*
> *my Constant Witness,*
> *my Shelter,*
> *my Best Friend,*
> *my Origin,*
> *my Dissolver of all my limitations,*
> *my Home,*
> *my Treasure House*
> *And The Seed Imperishable,*
> *And I am the tree.*

Bhagavad Gita 9:18

If you don't make a commitment to Source, you will be like a high-pressure hose spewing out energy in all directions with the potential to damage yourself and others. Only move forward if you can commit.

Your Spine Is a Center of Energy

These next exercises focus on the energy throughout your spine. It's important to associate this energy with the Word, which is the meditation on breath and the repeating of Hamsa.

Do this meditation;

Close your eyes. Focus on the movement of your breath, moving your diaphragm, repeating the Word. Take a minute to feel this rhythm.

Now bring your focus to your spine. Know that it is center of your energy field. Don't make any movements just feel your spine gently. Bring love to your awareness if you can and notice how this energy changes.

And with love, focus on your breath and notice the grounding it provides to the energy in your spine.

Continue to feel the spine and know it is a current of energy. It is a beautiful conductor of your Consciousness throughout your body. Your spine is the seat of your energy while spirit controls your body.

Continue to sit in meditation, doing the Word, breathing into your diaphragm. Bring love to your awareness.

When you're ready, come out of this meditation.

The Effulgence of a Thousand Suns.

<u>The Kundalini Shakti operates through the power of Hamsa</u>, *which is not different from the Self. Hamsa flows with the prana, and the prana flows through the nadis…<u>After Kundalini has awakened naturally, yoga takes place according to the inspiration of God</u>. It goes on in a spontaneous manner, while you go about your daily life. Kundalini is the energy which has created the entire universe, and when it is awakened within you, it works with its full power. From its seat at the base of the spine in the spiritual center known as muladhāra, it rises and begins to travel higher and higher, until it has reached the highest spiritual center, the sahasrāra, in the crown of the head. Moving within the body, it causes yoga postures and pranayama to take place spontaneously, as they are necessary. It purifies the blood and the bodily fluids and makes the body strong and free of disease. It stills the mind and focuses the attention within. Meditation occurs naturally, and knowledge arises on its own.*

As Kundalini unfolds, the inner world is revealed to you. Every day you have new realizations which fill you with wonder. On the outside, you can watch pictures on television, but when Kundalini works within, you see pictures inside, on the inner screen. Outside, you use the telephone. But on the inside, through the inspiration of Kundalini, you attain clairaudience. I am not telling you an amusing story. I am telling you what exists inside you. When you lose your inner worth, you become the slave of external things and lose the awareness of the inner world. But through the inner Shakti you come to know what truly exists within you.

Finally, as you pursue this self-born yoga, as the inner Shakti unfolds, you reach the sahasrara, the topmost spiritual center in the crown of the head. This is the culmination of your spiritual journey, and here the light of the Self reveals itself. In the sahasrara there is a divine effulgence. That light has the radiance of a thousand suns. In that center, there is no pain and no pleasure. Only the bliss of Consciousness exists there. In the center of that divine effulgence in the sahasrara, there is a tiny subtle blue light, which yogis call the mila bindu, the Blue Pearl. Watching this tender, infinitely fascinating light, you become aware of your true glory. Though smaller than a sesame seed, the Blue Pearl contains the entire universe. It is the light of God, the form of God within you. This is the divinity, this is the greatness, that lies within a human being. This is the true wonder of humanity. Therefore, perceive that light.

Just by looking at your face in the mirror, you will never know yourself. Only if you discover that light will you recognize who you really are. It was after seeing that light that the great ecstatic being Mansur Mastana said, "and'l-Hadd, I am God." After seeing that, the great Shankaracharya said, "I am Brahman, I am the Absolute." With the awareness of that, Jesus said, "The kingdom of God is within." God's kingdom does not lie only within Jesus or within these other great beings. It is inside you and inside me and inside everyone.

One day, in meditation, the tiny blue light, the light of the Self, expands to fill the universe, and then you experience your all-pervasiveness. You attain the state of the supreme Truth, the state beyond all pain and pleasure. You experience the true bliss of Consciousness. You know without any doubt, "I am God, and God is me.'" From then on, you live in constant awareness of the Self, in the state of perfect fearlessness and freedom.
    -Swami Muktananda; I am That

Rise My Friend

This is a different type of exercise from the others in this book. Take your time with it. It could be done over a day or it could be the focus of your meditation over several weeks. Whatever suits you. It simply can't be rushed, as it is a transformation - from a caterpillar to a butterfly.

It is very tricky to raise someone's energy like this through a book, yet what's provided is a safe method that uses Being states. But there are consistent warnings throughout just as a precaution in case you encounter latent energy or blockages. It is simply designed to give you a taste of this energy and is not meant as a substitute for a teacher or Master who can give you this power firsthand.

Here we utilize our chakras, which are real energy centers in the body. It is our own Consciousness with central points of energy that coalesce as nerve centers. They each have emotional functions that impact our lives through how we think, speak, and act.

The Root Chakra

In Sanskrit the root chakra is known as the *muladhāra chakra*, and is at the base of the spine. *Mula* means root, while *adhara* means base. When it is healthy, functioning well, and open you will be grounded, feel secure, and have courage. After each chakra is explained we will get you to focus on the associated Being states as a way of empowering that aspect of your energy.

As you do this exercise you may experience energy in the spine. If anything is uncomfortable, no problem, just begin breathing slowly through your nose and into your diaphragm doing the Word, exactly as you would for your meditation practice. If you experience uncomfortable energy in the base of your spine, bring your awareness to the top of your head. This is as a means of conducting your energy to balance it out if need be. If it persists gently touch the top of your head.

Grounded Being State

Feel the energy at the base of the spine and say, *I am Being grounded.*

Below, write down the first answer that comes to your mind. Don't think about it too hard.

With this Being state describe how you are thinking?
_____
_____
_____

With this Being state what are you saying?
_____
_____
_____

With this Being state how are you acting? What are you doing?
_____
_____
_____

Secure Being State

Feel the energy at the base of the spine and say, *I am Being secure.*

Below, write down the first answer that comes to your mind. Don't think about it too hard.

With this Being state describe how you are thinking?

_____
_____
_____

With this Being state what are you saying?

_____
_____
_____

With this Being state how are you acting? What are you doing?

_____
_____
_____

Courageous Being State

Feel the energy at the base of the spine and say, *I am Being courageous.*

Below, write down the first answer that comes to your mind. Don't think about it too hard.

With this Being state describe how you are thinking?

_____
_____
_____

With this Being state what are you saying?

_____
_____
_____

With this Being state how are you acting? What are you doing?

_____
_____
_____

Summary

When you have completed the above exercises, summarize by saying, *Aham Brahmasmi: I am grounded, I am secure, I am courageous.*

Then, with your eyes closed, visualize an orb or ball of light outside of you. Let this ball of light represent the energy at the base of your spine.

Repeat several times, *Aham Brahmasmi: I am grounded, I am secure, I am courageous.*

If you experience any uncomfortable energy surges, or dizziness, quit immediately. To reground yourself, return to a normal meditation practice focusing on any proclamation that suits you. If you return to this exercise and continue to experience any of the above, it means there are unresolved emotional issues creating energy blockages in that chakra.

I would then recommend returning to the practices in chapter three and come back to this exercise when you feel ready.

If you were comfortable, or experienced an energy surge but maintained your balance by taking full breaths in your diaphragm, then move forward.

The Sacral Chakra

In Sanskrit it is known as the *swadhisthana chakra* and is located just below the naval. *Swadhisthana* means abode of the Self, as in the base of the condensed spirit Self (the orb you that is the thinking, feeling, and Being Consciousness that is refracted in the body). When the chakra is healthy, functioning well, and open you will feel pleasure, flow with life, and your emotions will be guided in a healthy manner.

Again, if anything is uncomfortable, no problem, just begin breathing slowly through your nose and into your diaphragm, doing the Word, exactly as you would for your meditation practice. If you experience uncomfortable energy in the lower area of your spine, bring your awareness to the top of your head. If it persists gently touch the top of your head.

Passionate Being State

Feel the energy below your naval along the spine and say, *I am Being passionate.*

Below, write down the first answer that comes to your mind. Don't think about it too hard.

With this Being state describe how you are thinking?

With this Being state what are you saying?

With this Being state how are you acting? What are you doing?

The Expression of Vitality Being State

Feel the energy below your naval along the spine and say, *I am Being the expression of vitality.*

Below, write down the first answer that comes to your mind. Don't think about it too hard.

With this Being state describe how you are thinking?

With this Being state what are you saying?

With this Being state how are you acting? What are you doing?

Emotionally Healthy Being State
==

Feel the energy below your naval along the spine and say, *I am Being emotionally healthy.*

Below, write down the first answer that comes to your mind. Don't think about it too hard.

With this Being state describe how you are thinking?

_____
_____
_____

With this Being state what are you saying?

_____
_____
_____

With this Being state how are you acting? What are you doing?

_____
_____

Summary
==

When you have completed the above exercises, recall that you are the Universe. Remember Bhakti and your commitment to your Source, to the Light, to the God that you are.

Say, *Aham Brahmasmi: I am grounded, I am secure, I am courageous, I am passionate, I am the expression of vitality, I am emotionally healthy.*

Then, with your eyes closed, visualize an orb or ball of light outside of you. Let this ball of light represent the energy along your spine. Now see it gently and slightly move up from the base of your spin up along it to just below the naval.

Repeat several times, *Aham Brahmasmi: I am grounded, I am secure, I am courageous, I am passionate, I am the expression of vitality, I am emotionally healthy.*

If you experience any uncomfortable energy surges, or dizziness, quit immediately. To reground yourself, return to a normal meditation practice focusing on any proclamation that suits you. If you return to this exercise and continue to experience any of the above, it means there are unresolved emotional issues creating energy blockages in that chakra. I would then recommend returning to the practices in chapter three and come back to this exercise when you feel ready.

If you were comfortable, or experienced an energy surge but maintained your balance by taking full breaths in your diaphragm, then move forward.

The Solar Plexus Chakra

In Sanskrit it is known as the *manipura chakra* and is located at the solar plexus. *Mani* means shining or gem, while *pura* is place, thus place of the shining gem. When it's open, healthy, and flowing, we have self-esteem and feel personal power.

Again, if anything is uncomfortable, no problem, just begin breathing slowly, through your nose and into your diaphragm, doing the Word, exactly as you would for your meditation practice. If you experience uncomfortable energy in the lower and mid-area of your spine, bring your awareness to the top of your head. If it persists gently touch the top of your head.

Confident Being State

Feel the energy along the spine at your solar plexus and say, *I am Being confident.*

Below, write down the first answer that comes to your mind. Don't think about it too hard.

With this Being state describe how you are thinking?
___
___

With this Being state what are you saying?
___
___

With this Being state how are you acting? What are you doing?
___
___

Filled With Personal Power Being State

Feel the energy along the spine at your solar plexus and say, *I am Being filled with personal power.*

Below, write down the first answer that comes to your mind. Don't think about it too hard.

With this Being state describe how you are thinking?
___
___

With this Being state what are you saying?
___
___

With this Being state how are you acting? What are you doing?
___
___

Summary

When you have completed the above exercises, recall that you are the Universe. Remember Bhakti and your commitment to your Source, to the Light, to the God that you are.

Say, *Aham Brahmasmi: I am grounded, I am secure, I am courageous, I am passionate, I am the expression of vitality, I am emotionally healthy, I am confident, I am filled with personal power.*

Then, with your eyes closed, visualize an orb or ball of light outside of you. Let this ball of light represent the energy along your spine. Now see it gently and slightly move up from just below your navel to just behind your solar plexus.

Repeat several times, *Aham Brahmasmi: I am grounded, I am secure, I am courageous, I am passionate, I am the expression of vitality, I am emotionally healthy, I am confident, I am filled with personal power.*

If you experience any uncomfortable energy surges, or dizziness, quit immediately. To reground yourself, return to a normal meditation practice focusing on any proclamation that suits you. If you return to this exercise and continue to experience any of the above, it means there are unresolved emotional issues creating energy blockages in that chakra.

I would then recommend returning to the practices in chapter three and come back to this exercise when you feel ready.

If you were comfortable, or experienced an energy surge but maintained your balance by taking full breaths in your diaphragm, then move forward.

The Heart Chakra

In Sanskrit it is known as the *anahata chakra*, and is located at the heart, and behind it along the spine. *Anahata* means the unstruck, as in the unstruck sound, the space of Consciousness before forms are created, the Absolute in the heart of the human, in the heart of our Being. When it is open, healthy, and flowing we have self-love, and are loving ourselves fully. And we will have healthy flowing and satisfying relationships with a heart full of compassion for others naturally. We will forgive and not hold onto the past, allowing ourselves to love again, with no fear.

Again, if anything is uncomfortable, no problem, just begin breathing slowly, through your nose and into your diaphragm, doing the Word, exactly as you would for your meditation practice. If you experience uncomfortable energy in the lower and mid-area of your spine, bring your awareness to the top of your head. If it persists gently touch the top of your head.

Loving Ourselves Fully Being State

Feel the energy along the spine behind the heart and say, *I am Being fully in love with myself.*

Below, write down the first answer that comes to your mind. Don't think about it too hard.

With this Being state describe how you are thinking?
_____
_____
_____

With this Being state what are you saying?

With this Being state how are you acting? What are you doing?

Full of Compassion for Others Being State

Feel the energy along the spine behind the heart and say, *I am Being full of compassion for others.*

Below, write down the first answer that comes to your mind. Don't think about it too hard.

With this Being state describe how you are thinking?

With this Being state what are you saying?

With this Being state how are you acting? What are you doing?

Let's briefly review the *Five Keys of Enlightenment*, and as we do reflect on your experience with them.

1) Bhakti
2) Beyond Duality/Beyond Time
3) Identity: Ahum Brahmasmi

4) Pure Heart
5) There is No I

Do you feel a connection with the exercises we just did in this section and the *Five Keys of Enlightenment*?

Summary

When you have completed the above exercises, recall that you are the Universe. Remember Bhakti and your commitment to your Source, to the Light, to the God that you are.

Say, *Aham Brahmasmi: I am grounded, I am secure, I am courageous, I am passionate, I am the expression of vitality, I am emotionally healthy, I am confident, I am filled with personal power. I am in love with myself fully, I am full of compassion for others.*

Then, with your eyes closed, visualize an orb or ball of light outside of you. Let this ball of light represent the energy along your spine. Now see it gently and slightly move up from behind your solar plexus to behind your heart.

Repeat several times, *Aham Brahmasmi: I am grounded, I am secure, I am courageous, I am passionate, I am the expression of vitality, I am emotionally healthy, I am confident, I am filled with personal power. I am in love with myself fully, I am full of compassion for others.*

If you experience any uncomfortable energy surges, or dizziness, quit immediately. To reground yourself, return to a normal meditation practice focusing on any proclamation that suits you. If you return to this exercise and continue to experience any of the above, it means there are unresolved emotional issues creating energy blockages in that chakra.

I would then recommend returning to the practices in chapter three and come back to this exercise when you feel ready.

If you were comfortable, or experienced an energy surge but maintained your balance by taking full breaths in your diaphragm, then move forward.

The Throat Chakra

In Sanskrit it is known as the *vishuddha chakra*, located at the adam's apple for men, and the center of the throat in the neck for woman. *Vishuddha* means purity, as in when this chakra is open we express our purity. When it is open, healthy, and flowing, we are able to speak our truth from our hearts easily in kind and thoughtful ways, and listen to others.

Again, if anything is uncomfortable, no problem, just begin breathing slowly, through your nose into your diaphragm, doing the Word, exactly as you would for your meditation practice. If you experience uncomfortable energy in the upper area of your spine, bring your awareness to the top of your head, and base of your spine. If it persists gently touch the top of your head.

Speaking From Our Heart Being State

Feel the energy in your throat and say, *I am Being from my heart as I speak to others.*

Below, write down the first answer that comes to your mind. Don't think about it too hard.

With this Being state describe how you are thinking?
_____
_____
_____

With this Being state what are you saying?
_____
_____
_____

With this Being state how are you acting? What are you doing?
_____
_____
_____

Speaking Truthfully Being State

Feel the energy in your throat and say, *I am Being truthful from my heart as I speak to others.*

Below, write down the first answer that comes to your mind. Don't think about it too hard.

With this Being state describe how you are thinking?
_____
_____
_____

With this Being state what are you saying?

With this Being state how are you acting? What are you doing?

Kindly Listening Being State

Feel the energy in your throat and say, *I am Being a kind listener to others.*

Below, write down the first answer that comes to your mind. Don't think about it too hard.

With this Being state describe how you are thinking?

With this Being state what are you saying?

With this Being state how are you acting? What are you doing?

Summary

When you have completed the above exercises, recall that you are the Universe. Remember Bhakti and your commitment to your Source, to the Light, to the God that you are.

Say, *Aham Brahmasmi: I am grounded, I am secure, I am courageous, I am passionate, I am the expression of vitality, I am emotionally healthy, I am confident, I am filled with personal power. I* am in love with myself fully, I am full of compassion for others, I am speaking my heart to others, I am speaking my truth to others, I am listening kindly to others.

Then, with your eyes closed, visualize an orb or ball of light outside of you. Let this ball of light represent the energy along your spine. Now see it gently and slightly move up from behind your heart to your throat.

Repeat several times, *Aham Brahmasmi: I am grounded, I am secure, I am courageous, I am passionate, I am the expression of vitality, I am emotionally healthy, I am confident, I am filled with personal power. I am in love with myself fully, I am full of compassion for others, I am speaking my heart to others, I am speaking my truth to others, I am listening kindly to others.*

If you experience any uncomfortable energy surges, or dizziness, quit immediately. To reground yourself, return to a normal meditation practice focusing on any proclamation that suits you. If you return to this exercise and continue to experience any of the above, it means there are unresolved emotional issues creating energy blockages in that chakra.

I would then recommend returning to the practices in chapter three and come back to this exercise when you feel ready.

If you were comfortable, or experienced an energy surge but maintained your balance by taking full breaths in your diaphragm, then move forward.

The Third Eye Chakra

In Sanskrit it is known as the *ajna chakra*, located in the brain, between the eyebrows but a little above. *Ajna* means command, as in to command the Universe by Visioning in your mind's eye, your third eye, what you desire. When it is open, flowing, and healthy, we are not just open to other perspectives, but also to other frames of reference of reality. We can also see the light of our spirit, can access other realms, and can receive access to all knowing.

Again, if anything is uncomfortable, no problem, just begin breathing slowly through your nose and into your diaphragm, doing the Word, exactly as you would for your meditation practice. If there is any discomfort in your mind, or dizziness, bring your awareness to the bottom of your spine. If it persists sit in a meditation posture and place your hands on the ground, while doing the Word.

Open to Other Frames of Reference of Reality Being State

Feel the energy at your third eye and say, *I am Being open to other frames of reference of reality.*

Below, write down the first answer that comes to your mind. Don't think about it too hard.

With this Being state describe how you are thinking?

_____
_____

With this Being state what are you saying?

_____
_____

With this Being state how are you acting? What are you doing?

_____
_____

Let's briefly review the *Five Keys of Enlightenment*, and as we do reflect on your experience with them.

Again, review the *Five Keys of Enlightenment*, but this time, as you reflect on your experience with them, casually bring your focus to your third eye.

1) Bhakti
2) Beyond Duality/Beyond Time
3) Identity: Ahum Brahmasmi
4) Pure Heart
5) There is No I

Did you feel a connection with your third eye and the *Five Keys of Enlightenment*?

Summary

When you have completed the above exercises, recall that you are the Universe. Remember Bhakti and your commitment to your Source, to the Light, to the God that you are.

Say, *Aham Brahmasmi: I am grounded, I am secure, I am courageous, I am passionate, I am the expression of vitality, I am emotionally healthy, I am confident, I am filled with personal power. I am in love with myself fully, I am full of compassion for others, I am speaking my heart to others,*

I am speaking my truth to others, I am listening kindly to others. I am open to other frames of reference of reality.

Then, with your eyes closed, visualize an orb or ball of light outside of you. Let this ball of light represent the energy along your spine, to the back of your neck, and connected to the back of your skull. Now see it gently and slightly move up from your throat to your brain just behind your eyebrows and a little above.

Repeat several times, *I am grounded, I am secure, I am courageous, I am passionate, I am the expression of vitality, I am emotionally healthy, I am confident, I am filled with personal power. I am in love with myself fully, I am full of compassion for others, I am speaking my heart to others, I am speaking my truth to others, I am listening kindly to others. I am open to other frames of reference of reality.*

If you experience any uncomfortable energy surges, or dizziness, quit immediately. To reground yourself, return to a normal meditation practice focusing on any proclamation that suits you. If you return to this exercise and continue to experience any of the above, it means there are unresolved emotional issues creating energy blockages in that chakra.

I would then recommend returning to the practices in chapter three, and come back to this exercise when you feel ready.

If you were comfortable, or experienced an energy surge but maintained your balance by taking full breaths in your diaphragm, then move forward.

Third Eye Meditation

Close your eyes. Let your self sit in the rhythm of your breath. Imagine you are outside on a field on a clear blue-sky day. Your sitting on the field meditating. When you're ready bring your focus to your third eye and point it at the sky. Now imagine it is like a beam shooting out into the sky and let that beam hit the sky and penetrate it. Now travel along your beam from your third eye, follow that beam all the way to the sky and see the hole it has penetrated in the blue sky. Your beam from your third eye has penetrated the sky and now go through the penetrated hole. Behind the sky is the Universe, outerspace, with all the starts and planets. Imagine your self flying around everywhere. You are free and limitless. Play here for as long as you desire.

(1 min)

When your ready, go back through the hole you came, follow the beam back to your third eye, back to you meditating on the field. When you are ready, come out of this meditation.

The Crown Chakra

In Sanskrit it is known as the *sahasrara chakra*, located right on top of the skull, at the crown. *Sahasrara* means thousand-petal lotus, as in when it is open, the light radiating from it is like a thousand-petal lotus. When it is open, flowing, and healthy, it manages our connection to divine energy, and provides the feeling we can do anything.

Again, if anything is uncomfortable, no problem, just begin breathing slowly, through your nose into your diaphragm, doing the Word, exactly as you would for your meditation practice. If there is any uncomfort in your mind, or dizziness, bring your awareness to the bottom of your spine. If it persists sit in a meditation posture and place your hands on the ground, while doing the Word.

Limitless Being State

Feel the energy at the crown of your head and say, *I am Being limitless.*

Below, write down the first answer that comes to your mind. Don't think about it too hard.

With this Being state describe how you are thinking?

With this Being state what are you saying?

With this Being state how are you acting? What are you doing?

Unity Being State

Feel the energy at the crown of your head and say, *I am Being Unity.*

Below, write down the first answer that comes to your mind. Don't think about it too hard.

With this Being state describe how you are thinking?

With this Being state what are you saying?

With this Being state how are you acting? What are you doing?

Omnipresent Awareness Being State

Feel the energy at the crown of your head and say, *I am Being Omnipresent Awareness.*

Below, write down the first answer that comes to your mind. Don't think about it too hard.

With this Being state describe how you are thinking?

With this Being state what are you saying?

With this Being state how are you acting? What are you doing?

Summary

When you have completed the above exercises, recall that you are the Universe. Remember Bhakti and your commitment to your Source, to the Light, to the God that you are.

Say, *Aham Brahasmi: I am grounded, I am secure, I am courageous, I am passionate, I am the expression of vitality, I am emotionally healthy, I am confident, I am filled with personal power. I am in love with myself fully, I am full of compassion for others, I am speaking my heart to others, I am speaking my truth to others, I am listening kindly to others. I am open to other frames of reference of reality, I am Being limitless. I am Being Unity.*

Then, with your eyes closed, visualize an orb or ball of light outside of you. Let this ball of light represent the energy along your spine, along the back of your neck, and connecting to the back of your skull. Now see it gently and slightly move up from inside your brain to on top of your crown.

Repeat several times, *Aham Brahasmi: I am grounded, I am secure, I am courageous, I am passionate, I am the expression of vitality, I am emotionally healthy, I am confident, I am filled with personal power. I am in love with myself fully, I am full of compassion for others, I am speaking my heart to others, I am speaking my truth to others, I am listening kindly to others. I am open to other frames of reference of reality, I am Being limitless. I am Being Unity.*

If you experience any uncomfortable energy surges, or dizziness, quit immediately. To reground yourself, return to a normal meditation practice focusing on any proclamation that suits you. If you return to this exercise and continue to experience any of the above, it means there are unresolved emotional issues creating energy blockages in that chakra.

I would then recommend returning to the practices in chapter three and come back to this exercise when you feel ready.

If you were comfortable, or experienced an energy surge but maintained your balance by taking full breaths in your diaphragm, then move forward.

All the gates of the body closed, the mind confined within the heart, having fixed his life-energy in the head, engaged in firm yoga; uttering the one-syllabled 'Om', Brahman, thinking of Me, he who departs, leaving the body, attains the Supreme Goal
Bhagavad Gita – Chapter 8, verse 12-13

Conduct a meditation on Om, which is written and pronounced as Aum. This is the sound of ultimate reality. While you speak out loud the elongated Aum on the exhale of each breath, see a white energy, sparkling, or shooting white flames out of the crown of your head. Feel the spot right at the top of the crown of the head and a little in the head, through the brain.

The Mystical Marriage

When you want to cross a river what do you do? You get a boat and then row the boat to the other bank of the river. Then when you go to the other side, if you don't jump off the boat and step onto the bank you have not crossed the river yet. You might as well have not bothered rowing across the river, fighting the current of the river. Just jump off the boat when you reach the other side. That is why you crossed the river in the first place. Don't stay on the boat.

When you want to cross the river then you need a boat and the boat, in this case, is books and knowledge. You need the knowledge to take you to the other side. When you reach the other side then you have to jump off the boat of knowledge and you need to experience the understanding of the other bank of the river. Knowledge is the boat, not the destination. Jumping off the boat is meditation and experiencing the Truth.

Most seekers of truth cross the river but still stay on the boat. They don't jump off the boat; they are really still on the other side of the river. They cling onto the boat.
   -Munindra Saheb

Only after Consciousness has been able to speak through you can you learn how to let go and merge mind with Consciousness; this is the great Mystical Marriage. The Mystical Marriage is when you live from a place of conscious awareness of the desire of your Consciousness, and act on it.

Love is your Consciousness and the intelligent awareness of your heart. It is a surrender to love but as Consciousness, as the thinker, imaginer, and Visioner - the Being

This is what true attainment is, this is the ultimate stage of Consciousness, when wisdom is given to you within, a flow from Being, guiding you in your development and process, providing wisdom from beyond your mind.

Of myself I do nothing, the Father that dwelleth in me He doeth all the works.
Complete abdication.
Not you at all.

Whatever you're doing now, abdicate.
Say; <i>It is not I but my Consciousness.</i>
Say; <i>It is God, my Source doing it through me.</i></p>

This is the practice, and the depth and intensity of your experience will come with time.

You are not the mind.
You own the mind but are not the mind.
There is no I.

Going Further

This is only a glimpse of what an actual Guru, Master, or spiritual teacher can provide with proper training and guidance. To experience the strength of the Word, Light, and your Rising, you need personal direction. From here on, if you're still desiring to learn and grow, then Vision a teacher in your life to help you. You don't know in what form they might come.

Living in the World but Not of It

Because the Self exists so naturally within you, the sadhana you do to find the Self should also be natural. It should not involve difficult austerities. It should not give trouble to your body. It should not take you away from your home or your family. It should not be an obstacle to your mundane activities. Because God is not different from the world, your sadhana should also include the world. You should be able to practice your sadhana in this very world, easily and with love. Although there are countless sadhanas, countless practices, the sadhana you follow should be a natural sadhana taught by a guide who knows that sadhana. Not only that, it should be a sadhana in which you experience something within. From the beginning you should be able to catch at least a glimpse of the Self, because only if you have recognized and experienced God can you pursue Him and eventually attain Him.
-Swami Muktananda; I am That

I hope you found this guidebook helpful. Discovering yourself is a lifelong endeavor, and this book can only be a tool, a guide, one of the many you will most likely use over your lifetime.

Truth isn't just something you awaken to, but also something you practice. Try to meditate every day if you can. Try and see all pains and problems as opportunities to create who you choose to Be. Live by your purpose. Vision the outcomes you desire in life. Most of all, enjoy life; life is *leela*, the play.

My Guru would say, *Don't take life too seriously.* Live from the intentions of love. See the Source in all and in everything around you. If you're stocking shelves at a warehouse, then see the products you stock as Source. If you're selling in retail, then see the products you sell, and the customers you sell to, as Source. This is the practice.

Be a Light unto the darkness and curse it not.

Choose Heart. Be Love.
Be your Being Living in the Absolute.

References

Do We Really Know Who We Are?

Bach, R. (2016). *Jonathan Livingston Seagull*.

Beach TV CSULB. (2018, March 26). *Remote Viewing and Statistical Validation* [Video]. YouTube. https://www.youtube.com/watch?v=YrwAiU2g5RU

Crick, F. (1982). *Life itself: Its Origin and Nature*. Simon & Schuster.

Einstein, A. (1929). *A Heuristic Viewpoint Concerning the Production and Transformation of Light*.

Herbert, N. (2011). *Quantum Reality: Beyond the New Physics*. Anchor.

Hoyle, F., & Wickramasinghe, C. (1982). *Evolution from Space: A Theory of Cosmic Creationism*. Simon & Schuster.
https://www.discovermagazine.com/mind/the-science-behind-coincidence

Kabir. (2002). Songs of Kabir; Translated by Rabindranath Tagore, Weiser Books

Loria, K. Neil deGrasse Tyson thinks there's a 'very high' chance the universe is just a simulation. (2016, April 26th). Yahoo https://finance.yahoo.com/news/neil-degrasse-tyson-thinks-theres130300649.html?guccounter=1&guce_referrer=aHR0cHM6Ly93d3cuZ29vZ2xlLmNvbS8&guce_referrer_sig=AQAAAL2VqYLRJBCTXysSm5LWvjqsBDcvF6ZI5fZ_CHHEm_Y5PwNKxKpGXdJGmw3rtvnXWeB2cUtcp0xATVdcOGDJV1-miFYfkowH8q23M2WFGq0fH2qbqibsNd5lMUn-JaN8ypqjLd7GaGXGDyCTePngpBKkeFcY9eSo5U7wG_4llJs

Muktananda, S. (2015). *I am that: The Science of Hamsa from the Vijnana Bhairava*. Siddha Yoga Publication.

Nathanson, R. (2021, March 31). *The Hard Science of Reincarnation*.
https://www.vice.com/en/article/jgqygg/hard-science-of-reincarnation-past-lives

Newberg, A., MD, & Waldman, M. R. (2009). *How God Changes Your Brain: Breakthrough Findings from a Leading Neuroscientist*. Ballantine Books.

Paturel, A. (2020, May 24). *The science behind coincidence*. Discover Magazine.

Plato, Lamb, W. R. M., Shorey, P., & Bury, R. G. (1961). Plato: Euthyphro. Apology. Crito. Phaedo. Phaedrus. 1914, T.p. 1966.

Powell, C. What is the Simulation Hypothesis? Why Some Think Life is a Simulated Reality. (2018, October 3). NBC News. https://www.nbcnews.com/mach/science/what-simulation-hypothesis-why-some-think-life-simulated-reality-ncna913926

Prigogine, I., Gregair, N. and Babbyabtz, A. "Thermodynamics of Evolution", Physics Today:25, 1972, p23-28.

Radhakrishnan, S. (2011). *The Principal Upanisads*. HarperCollins Publishers.

Sen, T. (2007). *Ancient Secrets of Success: For Today's World*. Omnilux Communications Inc.

Surviving Death, Ricki Stern, Netflix, 2021, *Netflix*.

Verny, T. R. (2021). *The Embodied Mind: Understanding the Mysteries of Cellular Memory, Consciousness, and Our Bodies*. Simon and Schuster

Waldman, S. (2005). *Beyond a Reasonable Doubt: Convincing Evidence of the Truths of Judaism*. Feldheim Publishers.

The Power of a Meditation Practice

Kabir. (2002). *Songs of Kabir; Translated by Rabindranath Tagore,* Weiser Books

Muktananda, S. (2015). *I am That: The Science of Hamsa from the Vijnana Bhairava*. Siddha Yoga Publication.

Newberg, A., MD, & Waldman, M. R. (2009). *How God Changes Your Brain: Breakthrough Findings from a Leading Neuroscientist*. Ballantine Books.

Radhakrishnan, S. (2011). *The Principal Upanisads*. HarperCollins Publishers.

Sen, T. (2007). *Ancient Secrets of Success: For Today's World*. Omnilux Communications Inc.

The Yoga Sutras of Patanjali. (1990). Integral Yoga Publications

The Ocean of the Mind

Kübler-Ross, E., & Kessler, D. (2007). *On Grief and Grieving: Finding the Meaning of Grief Through the Five Stages of Loss*. Simon and Schuster.

Radhakrishnan, S. (2011). *The Principal Upanisads*. HarperCollins Publishers.

Simpson, J. A. (2002). *Oxford English Dictionary: Version 3.0 : Upgrade Version*. Oxford University Press.

The Yoga Sutras of Patanjali. (1990). Integral Yoga Publications

Walsch, N.D. (1997). *Conversations with God, Book 1 Guidebook: An Uncommon Dialogue*. Hampton Roads Publishing Company.

Wilder, T. (2007). *The Cabala and the Woman of Andros: Two Novels*. Harper Perennial Modern Classics.

The Rising

Chidbhavananda, S. (1997). *The Bhagavad Gita*. Sri Ramakrishna Tapovanam

The Yoga Sutras of Patanjali. (1990). Integral Yoga Publications

Walsch, N.D. (1996). *Conversations with God: An Uncommon Dialogue*, TarcherPerigee.

We Are Creator Beings with the Power to Create Reality Through Visioning

Allen, J. (2018). *As a Man Thinketh*.

Bach, R. (2014). *Jonathan Livingston Seagull: The Complete Edition*. Simon and Schuster.

Cameron, J. (2002). *The artist's way: A Spiritual Path to Higher Creativity*. TarcherPerigee.

Chidbhavananda, S. (1997). *The Bhagavad Gita*. Sri Ramakrishna Tapovanam

Harris, R., Aisbett, B. (2014). *The Illustrated Happiness Trap: How to Stop Struggling and Start Living*. Shambhala.

Hesse, H. (1998). *Siddhartha*. Wyatt North Publishing, LLC.

Kafka, F. (2011). *The Zurau Aphorisms*. Random House.

Radhakrishnan, S. (2011). *The Principal Upanisads*. HarperCollins Publishers.

Redfield, J., & Adrienne, C. (1995). *The Celestine Prophecy: An Experiential Guide*. Random House.

Sawyer, K. *Synchronicity and the Search for Significance*. (2018, December). significancemagazine.com. https://rss.onlinelibrary.wiley.com/doi/pdf/10.1111/j.1740-9713.2018.01213.x

Vimuktananda, S. (1938). *Aparokshanubhuti: Or Self Realization of Sri Sankaracharya*. Vadanta Press & Bookshop

Walsch, N.D. (1996). *Conversations with God: An Uncommon Dialogue*, TarcherPerigee.

Made in the USA
Las Vegas, NV
20 July 2025